Cease-Fire on the Family

For My Family and Yours

CEASE-FIRE ON THE FAMILY
& the End of the Culture War

Douglas W. Kmiec

CRISIS BOOKS
1995

Contents

Preface

THIS IS A BOOK ABOUT AND FOR FAMILIES in the midst of a culture war.

The American family, like the nation of which it is a part, is caught in this war, and it wants out. Yet the way out depends upon a re-discovery and re-dedication to standards of personal and cultural virtue that seem naggingly elusive in a modern era that both yearns for, and resents, direction.

There is a way out. A way illustrated as much by ancient instruction as by common sense. But the repository of this wisdom and the principal agent of instruction is not law or politics but the family itself.

Personal and cultural virtue depend upon a restoration of the family—not the decisions of the U.S. Supreme Court or the extreme political agendas of the left or the right. Factional politics on or off the Court remains hopelessly ensnared in the assertion of competing "rights," when the nation desperately needs a revival of an understanding of duty. Political rhetoric dominated by "rights to life" vs. "rights to choose" or "rights to develop" vs. "rights to preserve" or "rights to worship" vs. "rights to be separated from religion" is the rhetoric of antagonism, not understanding. It is rhetoric designed to allure persons into selfishly "empowering" themselves as individuals—from the left, through politics, and from the right, through the free market—not into ennobling themselves with a sense of duty to family or community.

Families want to cry out for an end to the cultural carnage. They lack the words. The words may fail to come because we have forgotten them, or perhaps, in the back half of the 1990s, because we have never learned them. Basic instruction in what makes America tick, what makes families work has somehow been omitted from life's instruction manual for the "baby-boom" generation.

Unable to talk with one another. We shout. We insult. We war through categorical demand. And in keeping with the nature of this first televised generation, the cultural provocation, and resulting bloodshed, is electronically delivered to the living room of every home, every evening.

It's time for families to find the voice necessary to end this madness. It is time for a cultural cease-fire.

This is a book about how that can be *practically* achieved in the life of each family. Piercing divisive political rhetoric and clearing away the artificial images of culture war, this book:

- ☐ focuses on real life—your family's life;
- ☐ helps families avoid the anxiety-laden "fool's game" of trying to win victories in the media or law or politics;
- ☐ lays out in straight-forward terms the "mega-virtues" that bind us together as a nation;
- ☐ encourages families to make education a necessary extension of itself;
- ☐ supplies the missing vocabulary for the teaching of personal virtue within families;
- ☐ gives needed self-confidence to restore the family to its primary role in the formation of moral character, and ultimately, cultural virtue.

Throughout the book, analysis is matched with practical, concrete, family prescriptions or checklists. These functional materials are informed by a faith in God that does not exclude the non-believer, personal insight and experience, and a knowledge of philosophical first principles.

Most of all, the book is informed by a father of five children who earnestly desires an America at peace with itself for a family he loves.

D. W. K.
Notre Dame, Indiana
Summer 1995

Chapter 1
No More Culture War

WE ARE TOLD—OVER AND OVER—that America is in the midst of a culture war or that our nation is suffering from profound cultural decline. Over the past thirty years, there has been a "560% increase in violent crime; a 419% increase in illegitimate births; a quadrupling in divorce rates";[1] and on and on through equally grim statistics on single parent households, children on welfare or in poverty, ever-declining SAT scores or the "dumbing down" of curricula. This book does not take issue with these highly disturbing, but regrettably undeniable, empirical facts.

This book does deny that it must necessarily be so.

America need not be on a cultural collision course with itself. *We* can avoid the collision. Please note the emphasis is on *we*—you and me—primarily in our families and churches. In this, we cannot expect Congress or the Supreme Court or a new president to rescue us. Indeed, continuing to rely on these agents will only make matters worse. Cultural differences will always exist, but difference becomes hatred when the law denies family and church its primary role in character formation. When the law preempts the wisdom of father or mother or clergy or seeks to mold through a monolithic educational establishment deliberately alienated from these moral actors, it promotes cultural war and community suspicion and decline.

Newsweek's Kenneth Woodward aptly reminds us that in the classics "the cultivation of virtue makes individuals happy, wise, courageous, competent. The result is a good person, a responsible citizen and parent, a trusted leader, possibly even a saint."[2] This

---

1   William J. Bennett, "Quantifying America's Decline," *The Wall Street Journal* (March 15, 1993), p. A10.

2   Kenneth L. Woodward, "What Is Virtue?" *Newsweek* (June 13, 1994), p. 38.

book will not pretend to be a handbook to sainthood, but it does suggest that if five principles are observed much of the societal division that now plagues us in war-like fashion can be superseded, if not overcome.

First, there must be a recognition that neither law nor politics is the source of personal virtue, or in a larger sense, "cultural virtue"—that is, the common good. Indeed, the more the law tries to impose or coerce virtue, the more likely it is to instill the opposite, raise false expectations, and worsen social tension.

Second, the primary agents in pursuit of cultural and individual virtue must be close at hand, part of what I call the smaller sovereigns—church, school, workplace, *and especially the American family*. Virtue is not something legislated through "three strikes and you're out" sentencing laws or welfare reform. Such laws address symptoms. Virtue is something practiced one-to-one. The practice of virtue comes from the observing of responsible parent and upright clergy, the family's closely applied discipline and encouragement of good behavior, and, ultimately, in the doing—of making right choices in sometimes difficult situations.

Third, in a modern America where freedom is too easily confused with the selfishness of "autonomy" or individual want or "legal right," *cultural* virtue depends upon a re-dedication to what I call the "mega-virtues" that underlie the American endeavor: belief in God and a knowable truth.

Fourth, beyond the mega-virtues, we must re-learn within the family or, in some families, discover for the first time the personal cardinal virtues of prudence, temperance, courage, and justice.

Fifth, family expectation must match family reality. Families must actually perform their intended function as a source of love and emotional support, respect for others, and the taking of responsibility for actions.

Our cultural divisions have been unduly "nationalized," and thus artificially magnified, either through the media or Congressional legislation or Supreme Court opinion. These cultural tensions have become nearly unbearable as one faction or another has sought to enact morality into law, as if legal enactment or judicial pronouncement would somehow rectify moral shortcoming. It's time we fully understand that just as overturning *Roe v. Wade* will not bring the unborn back to life or even prospectively stop the killing (as state laws could then still authorize the practice); neither will the passage of FACE (the recently enacted Freedom to Access to Clinic Entrances Act) or FOCA (the pending Freedom of Choice Act) eliminate the moral anxiety over abortion.

While there is always some necessary overlap between law and morality, as law implicitly involves a moral claim by its command of obedience, few of us seem to fully appreciate any longer that law cannot force moral consensus or instill virtue or character.

That job—the formation of moral character—necessarily falls to the family and the assisting smaller sovereigns of church, school, and workplace. Perhaps, it is difficult to conceive of schools and employers as moral instructors because so much of their authority has been sapped by legal and government intrusion. Public schools have lost much of their instructive capacity by Supreme Court interpretation that either actually precludes, or is understood to preclude, all meaningful reliance upon God or religion in the school house. Even were those legal impediments removed, however, the very notion of a public school with a uniform curriculum imposed by a secular and distant government from top-down, and from which only the affluent can escape, is in necessary tension with the pluralistic nature of American religious commitment and the different paths to virtue that those commitments represent.

Employers too have found their authority over the moral actions of their employees curtailed by labor statutes or agreements that preclude employers from setting standards for behavior—after, and even during, work. For example, one of the nation's leading discount stores, Wal-Mart, at one time proclaimed their support for the family in the store handbook by making an extra-marital affair a basis for termination. Several employees so terminated, along with the state attorney general of New York, have sued Wal-Mart, on the theory that the "recreational activities" of employees is none of Wal-Mart's business. But why not? Wal-Mart markets its products with a special emphasis on family, friendliness, and assistance. Why should that friendliness and concern stop at helping one locate the aisle with the garden fertilizer, and not include whether employees are being responsible parents and faithful spouses, and thus, virtuous citizens participating in the community Wal-Mart seeks to serve?

But schools and employers cannot be reasonably expected to undertake character instruction when more primary moral educators (parents and the church) have been too reticent or intellectually unprepared to articulate the overarching—or mega-virtues—upon which the American proposition is founded. If churches fail to make plain the importance of belief in God for a virtuous life, Wal-Mart is no position to pick up the slack. So too parents that leave children with no workable sense of an objective right and wrong forfeit a duty that is poorly, if ever, rectified in public school or elsewhere.

It may be possible to pin some of this failing by the clergy or us as parents on our own distorted national or generalized perspective. But if we are honest, moral failings in our children often reflect insufficient or incomplete moral formation in ourselves. When the personal cardinal virtues of justice, temperance, courage, and prudence are unknown, little understood, or understood only abstractly, we are at a loss for words to speak with our children even as we may "feel" we know what actions are right or wrong.

We must do more than wallow in cultural anxiety or aggravate cultural war. A re-awakening of virtue through the American family can bring needed cultural cease-fire. The prospects for this often exist just beneath the surface. For example, a 1991 survey found that two-thirds of Americans believe "there is no such thing as absolute truth."[3] Yet, other surveys reveal that Americans overwhelmingly want their president to have an exemplary public and private life, suggesting that when matters become concrete or specific, standards are assumed and insisted upon. As Robert Royal writes: "[i]f the same group had been asked, 'is enslaving or discriminating against another person always wrong?' or 'Should you park in a handicapped space if you're not handicapped?' we might find that most Americans do indeed believe in personal and social absolutes."[4]

We can sharpen our focus of these social absolutes, and in the process restore personal and cultural virtue, but again it is up to *us*—as parents and as members of church congregations. To slightly paraphrase the poet, Dante:

> To a greater force, and to a better nature, we, free, are subject, and that creates the mind in us, which the heavens have not in their charge. Therefore if the present world go astray, the cause is in us, in us it is to be sought.

The present world is astray. In our families, we can bring it back.

---

3   The survey is cited in Robert Royal, "Return to Virtue," *The American Character* No. 7 (June 1994), p. 3.

4   *Id.*

Chapter 2
Avoiding the Fool's Game—The Mistaken Search for Virtue in Law and Politics

BRINGING AMERICA BACK toward virtue requires a positive vision of what can be achieved through the family and a skeptical, or at least realistic, view of what can*not* be achieved through law and politics. I'm no pollyanna. A lawyer's training is to see shortcomings, problems. What's more, our family has not gone untouched by "war"—or at least, senseless violence. My wife's brother lost his life in late 1992 at age 47 to a bullet at work, his lifeless body discovered next to an open, emptied safe. Our home set in the idyllic countryside of southwestern Michigan has been burglarized as has those of far too many of our neighbors. Divorce has also touched our family in ways we wish it had not. There is little question that the children from these "broken homes," to use a term that deserves more frequent and honest use, have had it rough-going, and are more difficult to instruct, and, for a subsequent step-parent, even at times to love.

There are *real* problems in the life of every American, mine and yours, but need families continue to engage in cultural war as the intellectuals claim?[1] No. We must not let ourselves be bullied or persuaded to maintain arms against each other—at least not in the sense, and on the particular battlefields, that have ensnared the American family over the last three decades (the courts, the Congress, the state legislatures). American families cannot afford to be distracted into playing a fool's game—the pursuit of truth and virtue principally, maybe even solely, through law and politics.

---

1   See Elizabeth Fox-Genovese, "Culture Wars, Shooting Wars," *First Things* (June/July 1994), p. 49.

The Limited Function of Law and Politics

The function of law is largely to keep the peace, to maintain order. In this, it is aimed most effectively at the control of conduct. The law is least effective when it tries to coerce belief. The law addresses external, not internal, man. While one hears the law described as a means of settling dispute, this is true to only a very limited extent. The law "settles" by employing a third party, usually a judge, to determine an outcome. If the judge has faithfully employed relevant legal precedents (the law as announced in prior statute or cases), his opinion is said to be "well-reasoned," and the result is, for all practical purposes, imposed on the parties. The dispute is "settled" in the sense that no authority will listen to it further and the loser must comply under *force* of law. Odds are, however, the losing side retains the belief that it is right. The law has failed to persuade. It often does.

Is politics more persuasive? The media attention given political campaigns might suggest that if law doesn't persuade or supply meaning, politics does. Yet, it is surely understatement to note that the nature of political debate is given to overstatement. Take, for example, the part of the GOP's "Contract with America" immodestly entitled the "American Dream Restoration Act." The Act would provide a pro-family $500 per child tax credit. As helpful as such attention to economic fairness is, even Newt Gingrich would likely admit (off-the-record) that the Act is only at the periphery of what ails American families.

In truth, even with a Congress re-invigorated by the unmistakable frustration expressed by millions of voters in the 1994 elections, politics is little more than a sorting or selection mechanism that precedes the law. Through the political process—candidate nomination, election, service, removal—we choose, not moral instructors, but administrators (be they called presidents, senators, congressmen or judges), who we think can best perform the law's function of maintaining order. A president, Supreme Court justice, or member of Congress may, on occasion, turn out to be a credible source of moral authority, but if that is so, it is not by reason of office, but the quality of the officeholder's prior moral training. As Robert Royal writes: "[p]olitics and politicians can probably do very little to promote these wide-ranging conceptions of the good. At present, it would be a step in the right direction if they stopped setting a bad example and started talking as if good and evil exist."[2] In an age where the president is being sued for sexual harassment and the electorally defeated, but once powerful, chairman of the House Ways and Means Committee is under indictment for the alleged embezzlement of government monies, that indeed would be a step in the right direction.

The Fool's Game

Now, some reading this will complain that these descriptions of law and politics are too narrow. The law, it will be claimed, is a great educator that must mirror moral judgment and bring us to virtue. Similarly, politics will be seen as the manifestation and constant redefinition of the nation's moral beliefs. These are sweeping assertions. They are also foolish. Neither law nor politics is up to the task of moral formation. Only the family, assisted by church, school, and workplace, can perform this function. Envisioning law and politics as primary moral educators merely aggravates cultural division. Take as an example the most explosive issue in the culture war: *Abortion.*

For the past twenty years, both sides have been petitioning the Supreme Court to settle the basic moral dispute over when life begins. Pro-life forces muster theological, scientific, and philosophical argument, and ask the Court, in essence, to insist that everyone *believe* that life begins at conception. Pro-abortion forces answer with medical, economic, and sociological argument, asking the Court to insist that everyone *believe* that unless a woman has the unfettered discretion to terminate a pregnancy, she is less than a whole person participating—in the words of the Court—in the "economic and social life of the nation."

Now both sides in the abortion debate may outwardly disclaim any interest in coercing belief. The pro-life side will contend that their interest is to prevent the *conduct* of the taking of life; those at the pro-abortion table will characterize their interest as precluding *conduct* that interferes with the woman's reproductive decisions. But, in fact, the purpose of both sides is to enlist whatever power or authority the Court has to insist that one side or the other, as a matter of belief, is correct.

What has this meant for the law? Less respect and less capacity to perform its assigned and envisioned function: the maintenance

---

2   Robert Royal, "Return to Virtue," *The American Character*, No. 7 (June 1994), p. 8.

of order. Nominees for the Supreme Court are analyzed not as fair arbiters of past decision or interpreters of constitution or statute, but on whether they have the proper "judicial philosophy"—viz. the "belief system" of the particular analyst or commentator. Thus, whether a judicial nominee is capable of performing a judge's intended and more limited task of faithfully and intelligently reading statutes, is largely ignored. And once judges are appointed based on belief rather than legal ability, the law itself is held in less respect. No longer is the law the collective judgment of democratic process and applied reason; it is force dressed in the words "case opinion."

The same is true of politics as well. Presidential and other elections at the national and even state level have become painful referenda on moral beliefs rather than the selection of capable executives and lawmakers. Capacity to govern within the limits of the law—that is, maintaining domestic order, a sound currency, a stable foreign policy, and a strong defense—has become secondary to a candidate's ability to rhetorically identify the right "mix" or "spin" of the beliefs of his constituency. Too frequently, a politics dominated by the rhetoric of belief, like a judiciary dominated by "judicial philosophy," fails to act or perform its intended function. It can "talk the talk" but not "walk the walk" of governing.

Worse, the high-profile campaigns to have law or politics reshape internal beliefs have misled families into mistaking the law's failure or politics's failure to succeed as their (i.e., the families') own. The reasoning proceeds: If the Supreme Court does not believe abortion is an immoral taking of life, then it must not be. If a presidential candidate articulates the belief that abortion should be a nationally subsidized medical expense, and that president is elected, then personal belief must accept abortion as no different than a tonsillectomy.

Utter nonsense? Families, you say, will continue to teach moral beliefs regardless of legal or political outcomes. Perhaps. Much of this book is devoted to helping families do just that. But, families get distracted when the law or politics too intrusively or too readily intervenes in the effort, and families get discouraged when the intervention cuts deeply against the grain of moral beliefs taught within the family. The distraction, and even the discouragement, is aided and abetted by both friend and foe of the family. Foes seek to coerce belief through law and politics that is antagonistic to the family. Friends emphasize in newsletters and letters soliciting funds to file briefs in law courts or run campaigns how the moral system of the family has been weakened by this or that legal ruling or a particular political opponent.

Does this mean the law and politics should stay out of moral questions? As much as possible, yes. It is, however, not always possible. Even a simple traffic law has some moral grounding. The sanctity of life is great enough that stoplights and the rules of the road are fully warranted. But lawyers and politicians, and especially families, since the previous two categories tend to forget, must always bear in mind that the law cannot prohibit every vice. The great moral thinker, Thomas Aquinas, once put it this way:

> The purpose of human law is to lead men to virtue, not suddenly, but gradually. Therefore, it does not lay upon the multitude of imperfect men the burdens of those who are already virtuous, viz., that they should abstain from all evil.[3]

The law, according to Aquinas, should forbid "only the more grievous vices, from which it is possible for the majority to abstain; and chiefly those that are injurious to others, without the prohibition of which human society could not be maintained."[4] Murder and theft come immediately to mind. This does not mean that other vices, those that do not directly injure others—such as the use of alcohol or tobacco[5]—are not wrongful; it merely means that we must carefully assess whether the law would do more harm than good in prohibiting such activities totally or even in specific ways or settings. Consider: the lawless, and often violent, defiance of the Prohibition era; the rash of "smokers vote" bumper stickers or the articulated resentment that smokers exhibit to mandated smoke-free zones. There are many contemporary examples of where the law runs the risk of being held in contempt for being at odds with the community's moral standards.

Yet, note two things. First, the mere fact that a law does not prohibit an activity does not mean that it is not wrongful or a vice. It is the high duty of families to educate sufficiently toward per-

---

3   St. Thomas Aquinas, *Summa Theologiae*, I-II, q. 95, a. 1.

4   *Id.* at q. 96, a. 2.

5   Obviously, alcoholism and the possible harms from secondary smoke, that is, being in the same room as a smoker, suggest that even the examples mentioned may not be without injury to others.

sonal virtue so that such activity is seen as morally improper. Second, the law does have a duty to prohibit the more "grievous vices." Of course, there will always be disagreement among individuals as to what should come within this category. Not surprisingly, the abortion controversy is one such example.

What then? First and foremost, families—aided by their particular religious instruction—must draw heavily upon the mega-virtues and cardinal virtues discussed later in this book in order to better understand and dedicate themselves to belief and conduct that is objectively right. In other words, the first duty is to educate, train, and if you will, legislate within one's own family and faith congregation. But families do live *in* larger communities too and they have a duty to share their learned wisdom in this larger setting. The most effective way to share such wisdom will be to practice it in personal action. But secondarily, it may also mean some prudent—as opposed to foolish—participation in law and politics.

To be prudent in the legal or political process, family members should be guided by a desire to persuade, recognizing that even if they can win the law to their side, it is impossible to compel the belief of another. With respect to moral and religious questions, as one writer put it, "no one can search for religious truth, hold religious beliefs, or act on them authentically, for someone else."[6] How true.

Nevertheless, as politics and the public's moral compass are pushed to be adjusted, by adding to or deleting from the list of "grievous vices" that should be prohibited by law (and obviously, this is what is afoot with abortion, homosexuality, contraception, assisted suicide, divorce, the use of drug, alcohol and tobacco, etc.), the contribution of families should be characterized by substance, not slogan. To ensure that substance governs, the following few "guidelines of respect" might usefully guide family participation:

Family Prescription

   * Don't be afraid to be counter-cultural in law or politics,
     but first, be counter-cultural in your own family.

There is plenty to be counter-cultural about. Every night the

---

6   Robert P. George, *Making Men Moral* (New York: Oxford, 1993), p.
     220.

evening newspaper is filled with murder and violence and dispute. Every day, the television spews forth with talk shows and soap operas that extol, display, even revel in perverted America or adulterous America or AIDS America. If this isn't the family or community that you live in, do you object by turning this distorted portrayal off and registering dissent with producers and station managers, or do you passively accept this distortion into your family home, with a complacent "oh well, this is the '90s"?

Schools too are finding it harder to teach. The best teachers are often those who resist fads or trends—who demand that homework not be a thing of the past, that school work not be dominated so much by the promotion of self-esteem as by the acquisition of basic skills and knowledge, that inflated, or so-called "re-centered," SAT scores and grades be set aside for candid, one-on-one evaluation, and so forth.

The world of work merits similar counter-cultural examination. Women now have the jobs men used to have and generally do them quite well. No surprise. But with both women and men in the marketplace, the children are literally home alone . . . or worse. Drug addicts and those suffering from contagious diseases demand, and get, employment under allegations of handicap discrimination. It is commonplace, if not legally required, to hire and promote on the basis of race or gender, even as there remains something gnawingly wrong with being directed to select employees on the basis of stereotype—even benign stereotype. The prolixity of law now makes the federal court every employer's branch office. Yet, few, if any, of these costly efforts satisfy anyone. Are we and our family members in the workplace letting this be known, or are we tolerating this as the "cost of doing business"?

Within the home, our families may be insufficiently counter-cultural as well. By not objecting to intrusive work schedules and organizational commitments, or even well-meaning or unthinking friends who make it difficult for family members to spend time together, we end up sacrificing our family's well-being. Two-income couples find it especially difficult to intersect. Eating a family meal is a rarity. And all the while, of course, the television preempts family time and discussion—even when nothing's on—thanks to the vcr.

In Nappanee, Indiana, not far from Notre Dame, the Amish are profoundly counter-cultural. They have no televisions, drive about in carriages, dress plainly, and live in closely knit, self-sustaining agricultural communities. Their very lives of wholesome responsibility and peacefulness stand as a powerful witness against the violence and decadence that surround them, even in such "livable" towns as nearby South Bend. This is not a call to be Amish necessarily, but might not all of our families benefit from an increased willingness to stand somewhat apart from modern culture? As we direct our families toward virtue, and then assist others in this pursuit by participating in legal or political discussion, there must be reasonable distance from what is rooted in vice and self-indulgence, but is nevertheless "accepted" as part of the culture.

This can be done easier than you think. For example, families can act as witnesses against explicit violence or inappropriate sexual activity or language in movies. Such witness might be accomplished by simply a "counter-cultural" expression of concern (e.g., telling the librarian or the video store or your neighbor or fellow church member). Along these lines, my wife and I recently were persuaded to see the movie *Forrest Gump*, starring actor Tom Hanks. On the surface, *Gump* is seemingly one of the more benign offerings of the day—compared, for example, to Oliver Stone's outrageously violent *Natural Born Killers*, and it has performed well at the box office and won numerous Academy Awards. Advertised to appeal to young people, our children have been lobbying to see it. We will decline, and advise others to do so as well, because the movie contains gratuitous sexual scenes, including one where Sally Fields, playing Forrest's mother, has sexual intercourse with the school principal in order to have Forrest admitted to school. The first amendment gives movie producers the freedom to denigrate motherhood, women and school authorities in this way, and the denigration may amuse some patrons in the theater. However, the same first amendment permits, and the pursuit of virtue invites, our family's responsible, counter-cultural expression of dissent.

Family Prescription

* **When being counter-cultural, be prepared to explain.**

In dissenting from modern culture, families must be sufficiently informed to explain their objection. For example, lawmaking bodies are presently debating whether to extend "domestic partnership" status to same-sex partners, or, in other words, to allow homosexual individuals to be considered "married" for purposes of public and private benefits, adoption, and the like. Such legislation is portrayed as ending a form of discrimination. No civil person should tolerate invidious discrimination, but is that what this is? An informed counter-cultural response might begin by suggesting how conflating heterosexual marriage with homosexual sodomy denies reality. Men and women are different, and in their difference, there is a necessary complementariness that is essential to procreation and child-rearing. So too the legislation, it might be said, confuses tolerance with approval. In this regard, families developing a serious counter-cultural response within a particular faith tradition might turn more explicitly to Biblical and religious instruction to illustrate the importance of maintaining proper sexual distinctions. Still others can raise concerns of public morality and health. In short, counter-cultural objection must be studied and well-thought-out. This takes time, not sound-bite or radio talk-show venom. How many of us have examined the sources of instruction in our churches and libraries to give real weight to counter-cultural objection? Too few, I'm afraid.

Of course, any studied, counter-cultural response to the aggressive push to recognize homosexuality as an alternative life style in *law* will truly be effective only if our personal behavior reflects the same principled response in *fact*. Homosexuality as a form of sexual gratification outside marriage is endorsed by divorces of convenience (the senior executive's "trophy wife," as Bill Bennett has called it), extra-marital affairs, and the tolerance of contraceptive sexual activity by our unmarried children. Homosexuality as a practice is furthered by a more common disregard of the channeling of sexual relations within marriage. There is a direct line to illegitimacy as well. As one writer has explained, "We could hardly turn to the poor and say, OK fellas, [sexual liberation] is fine for us, but not for you—*you* have to cleave to the straight and narrow. So we destigmatized for everybody much sexual behavior that formerly had been kept in check by strong social disapproval. In the case of the poor, we destigmatize getting pregnant out of wedlock, even for fifteen year olds, even for thirteen year olds."[7]

Family Prescription

  * When being counter-cultural, don't provoke.

---

7   Myron Magnet, *The Dream and the Nightmare* (New York: William Morrow, 1993).

From the above, it should be patent that being counter-cultural in legal or political discussion is not the same as guerrilla warfare. It can be difficult to avoid inflammatory or sweeping rhetoric when dearly held first principles are at stake, but their avoidance is the only possible means toward persuasion. And when a family devotes valuable family hours to participate in legal or political matters, persuasion—not provocation—should be the whole point. These opportunities to influence are not the equivalent of football pep-rallies where the approval of the crowd is assured upon the recitation of the proper cheer.

There are cultural aggravations in America, but they only result in a war, when families adopt rules of engagement that delegate to law and politics the primary duty to set the moral course. If moral issues are forced into court or politics, especially if they are pressed in these forums prematurely, the family diverts needed time away from reaffirming moral teaching within itself. Without this reaffirmation, the American family completes the fool's game by fulfilling the prophecy of cultural war. How? By suffering actual losses in court and at the polls and then by being as lost, disconnected, and unhappy within the family as the culture war proponents describe. Unhappy as spouse (see the divorce rate), unhappy as child (see the rate of adolescent crime, drug use and teen suicide), unhappy as employer (see the *Wall Street Journal*), and unhappy as citizen (see a large number of defeated Democratic members of Congress). Even Hillary Rodham Clinton, distracted by politics from the duties of the "first family," yearns for "a politics of meaning."

The search for meaning, purpose, virtue. It is more than nostalgia for days past. As one writer put it, "Americans with a purely secular view of life have too much to live with, too little to live for. Everything is permitted and nothing is important. But once growth and prosperity cease to be their reason for existence, they are bound to ask questions about the purpose and meaning of their lives: Whence? Whither? Why?"[8]

Where do we come from? Where are we going? Why? American families cannot allow the culture war proponents to convince us that either we lack answers to these questions or that they lie exclusively or even predominantly in politics or law. The answers to these questions are found first, by ending the fool's game—that

---

8   Os Guinness, *The American Hour* (New York: Free Press, 1993) p. 398.

is, de-emphasizing what is remote or secondary (politics, law), and embracing what's real and primary (the one-to-one instruction of parent to child, minister to church member). If that instruction builds upon the mega-virtues of belief in God and a knowable truth and the cardinal virtues of prudence, courage, temperance, and justice, it is capable of genuinely sustaining personal, family and civic life.

Chapter 3
Distinguishing the Real from the Artificial

UNDERSTANDING THAT VIRTUE is not derived from law or politics supplies a realistic appraisal of forces external to the family. It is equally important to draw necessary distinctions between the real and the artificial within the family. That's what this chapter is about, and the best place to begin is with the greatest imposter of them all: the televised distortion of modern life. No family today can direct itself toward virtue without the unequivocal recognition (to be often repeated):

Life is Not TV

Vice is news; virtue is not. Violence is news; gentleness is not. Victims (of child abuse, of sexual harassment, of legal claims newly minted every day) is news; getting along, forgiveness, understanding of error is not. That which is portrayed in news and much entertainment tends to be negative, destructive of community. By contrast, most family members spend their daily lives trying to be constructive, at home, on the job, in school, in church congregation.

Outside the electronic box in the living room, the world of families and neighbors and co-workers exists largely intact, and that is where, thankfully, we principally interact. Yet, the mass media distortion has its effect. We do not look upon strangers, as the words of one song puts it, "with innocent eyes." Instead, we see danger, threat, and cultural disintegration. We fall prey to, and become hardened by, the anecdotes of culture war. To be sure, some strangers do wish us harm, and the index of cultural indicators verifies that rates of illegitimacy and crime, not academic performance, are on the rise.[1] Yet, for most of us on this day and

---

1   William Bennett, "Index of Leading Cultural Indicators," Vol. I (Empower America, The Heritage Foundation, Free Congress Foundation, March 1993).

every day, the culture war of violence and abortion and homosexuality remains largely a "televised" phenomenon. But be careful! If left unchecked, what one sees may well be what one gets. If enough generations of family members grow up with Geraldo and Oprah and Jenny Jones as their primary moral instructors, then vice, not virtue, almost certainly will be just around the corner.

That this concern with the media is not exaggeration may be illustrated in a number of ways. First, consider some of the subjects presented on Geraldo: "Gang Rape," "Kids Who Kill," "Teenage Sex Offenders," "Teens Trade Sex for Dope," and "Children Who Kill Their Children."[2] Second, in shows popular with adolescents, "rates of [portrayed] sexual contact have increased 21% since comparable data were gathered in 1982, and 103% since 1980."[3] These shows are not without their actual effect. "Well-controlled laboratory studies, building on earlier research, show[ed] that viewing violent television [leads] to aggressive behavior on the part of both children and adolescents. . . . Field studies of young children and adolescent boys demonstrate[d] deteriorations in self-control and increases in interpersonal aggression."[4] By inundating the family living room with these and similar images, the television stranger effectively kidnaps the child into the harshest depictions of the adult world. As one writer put it, television undercuts the very concept of childhood by abolishing differences between adults and children "with respect to dress, games, language and sexuality."[5]

Family Prescription

> * Evict the television stranger—or at least carefully ration his visiting hours.

2   Lynette Friedrich Cofer and Robin Smith Jacobitz, "The Loss of Moral Turf: Mass Media and Family Values," in *Rebuilding the Nest*, eds. David Blankenhorn, Steven Bayme, and Jean Bethke Elshtain (Milwaukee, Wis., 1990), p. 193.

3   *Id.* at 192, citing "Sex Content in R-rated Films Viewed by Adolescents," Technical Report No. 3 (Michigan State University Department of Telecommunications) (1986).

4   *Id.* at 197, citing among other studies, "TV Violence and Viewer Aggression: A Cumulation of Study Results, 1956–1976," *Public Opinion Quarterly*, 41 (1977), pp. 314–31; Lynette Friedrich-Cofer and Aletha Huston, "Television Violence and Aggression: The Debate Continues," *Psychological Bulletin* 100 (1986), pp. 364–71.

5   *Id.* at 191, citing Neil Postman, *The Disappearance of Childhood* (New York: Delacorte Press, 1982).

The best antidote to media distortion is, of course, to avoid it. Turn off the television set! Expel the television stranger. If that's too hard, we owe it to ourselves and our family to make explicit and frequent editorial warnings, not unlike that on the sides of cigarette packages: *The contents of this electronic package are hazardous to family health.* In short, we must be honest with ourselves and our family, and pray each day a prayer of gratitude, that television bears little relation to what is actually happening in the daily life of our family.

If the television stranger—as a practical matter—continues to be a part of a family's life, it ought to be pursued cautiously together. Viewing ought to be limited to a favorite program and watched as a family, with parents pointing out what is and is not real. Commenting as the show progresses allows many moral object lessons, since the shows are filled with cohabitation, adultery, murder, deception and the like. After the show, ask how particular characters might have acted better or how one of your children would have responded to the situation portrayed.

Family Prescription

  * Concentrate on news of the local community or
    neighborhood.

In terms of news, it is helpful to turn the family's news focus from the national to the local and personal. The media itself is an unduly nationalizing influence, so reducing TV consumption generally helps here as well. This is certainly true of television, but frequent travelers know that the bulk of local newsprint also consists of little more than lightly edited versions of national news wire stories. The reality needed to nurture personal or cultural virtue is more likely to be grasped if a family can identify items in the evening newspaper that might really affect a family member in a direct way, say, those announcing a change in school curriculum or worthwhile local activities for the family (fairs, plays, volunteer opportunities).

Family Prescription

  * Restore real functions for the family.

Families Need Functions. Having turned off the television and refocused on events in the home or closer to it, members of the family—especially the younger ones—are likely to say, all right what do we do now? Plenty! To begin with, families can pick up the conversations that have been interrupted or stopped for years by the television stranger. Ever observe your family watching TV? They aren't interacting; they're barely moving. Oh, there may be a groan over a missed touchdown and the like, but if anyone really tries to converse, they are promptly silenced and thought impolite. A child development expert once summarized what family members are *not* doing when they watch television. They are not:

* Scanning
* Practicing motor skills, gross or fine
* Practicing eye-hand coordination
* Using more than two senses
* Asking questions
* Exploring
* Exercising initiative or motivation
* Being challenged
* Solving problems
* Thinking analytically
* Exercising imagination
* Practicing communication skills
* Being either creative or constructive[6]

With the television in the off position, families discover what happened during the day at school, at work, or around the home. Meals are unimpeded by distraction. Letters can be written to grandparents or friends far from home base, and letters received can be read aloud. Other "active" forms of entertainment from touch football to family baseball to "rainy day" card playing, checkers, and charades can be enjoyed. Instead of watching others slam-dunk, junior can show Dad how he "grabs rim" outside in the driveway. Have you ever noticed that the best gifts on holidays or birthdays are the one's Dad and Mom are willing to play or be involved with? This principle can be applied to a great variety of family functions generally and throughout the year. Hammer, nail, and scrap wood can be combined to make the craziest things and

---

6   John Rosemond, "Children and Television," *Boston Globe* (January 3, 1984), cited in Rahima Baldwin, *You Are Your Child's First Teacher*, at 296 (Berkeley, Cal.: Celestial Arts, 1989), p. 29.

result in some of the best memories. Somewhere among the Christmas ornaments in our basement is a small wooden "sleigh" my children and I fashioned out of leftover materials from a home repair. Few probably can identify it as a sleigh without prompting, but it means more to me and the children than even a string of lights that actually work.

And family activity or function in lieu of television need not be all entertainment. Obviously, time can and should be spent on homework or involving children in the cooking of meals or the running of the home. Parents are often reluctant to involve children in fix-up tasks or the bookkeeping involved in running a small family business out of a fear that the work will not be done correctly. "What do children know?" ask parents. But the better question is, "What will children ever know [or learn], if parents fail to ask children to attempt these things?" And by the way, if we are honest with ourselves and our children, half the time we don't know what we're doing at first, either. Why not learn together? Recently, for example, after close to 42 years of life, I installed my very first pair of wooden window shutters. Ever do that? It's harder than it looks. For weeks, the brackets and screws and hinges awaited my attention, in part, because our small scroll saw didn't seem quite up to the task of trimming the shutters to fit the interior of the window frame. When the weekend rolled around I summoned enormous courage and my ten year old, and we went to it. It took a while—several hours, actually—so long that my oldest daughter went outside to peer into the window to see what we were up to. We finished eventually, and the shutters open and close well enough, and were you to come visit, we'd ask you to nod your approval while walking by them quickly. But whether our shutters merit raves or, if you will, "shudders," they're ours—a work done together by father and son, and that means more than their somewhat imperfect appearance—or at least, so I've explained to my wife.

During the first days with the television off, some families may experience the attempted "escape" phenomenon. This occurs when some family member, usually an adolescent child, adjusts to the disappearance of TV at home by disappearing himself to the home of a friend, where lo and behold, the TV stranger is alive and well. Children aren't the only culprits here, as Mom or Dad may seek escape at the movies or a friend's house.

The escape phenomenon should be resisted. TV in any location reintroduces artificial life and distracts from the real. If good, virtuous behavior is our goal, it is not enough to say "turn off the television" or "go read a book." Mothers and fathers must commit not only to avoid the misleading saturation of the media but also actively to substitute every-day functions for it, be it playing catch, changing the oil, cutting the lawn, or singing songs and praying together. We have found that planting a garden can supply a great deal of enjoyment together. Every child can raise and care for their own crop throughout the summer, a task which instills both responsibility (watering and weeding have to be done periodically), and a sense of contribution and accomplishment as the harvest is shared at meals. My daughter is delighting in trying to teach her tone-deaf father how to play the piano. While I haven't advanced beyond a few lines of "This Land Is Your Land," she has proven to be a delightful and encouraging teacher.

Family Prescription

* **Designate family times.**

Certainly, it will not be possible for family members to be together at all hours on every day. Parents and children have separate work and school obligations and do need time alone. But, in point of fact, the television stranger has been creating "aloneness" and isolation for some time. To counteract that, it is wise to create designated "family times," say during all or part of weekends or after certain hours of the day. At these times, everyone is asked to be present in the home and to undertake the family's various common pursuits of work, worship, entertainment, or simple conversation.

The nice thing about "family times" is that, after they become well established, they create real contentment and immunity from the invading world at large. In our household, meal times are family times, and while the telephone frequently rings just as we are about to devour the first bite, we have allowed another electronic device, the telephone answering machine, to keep us gathered and undisturbed. Weekends in our household are expected to revolve around the activities of each other. So too, if our ten year old has a little league or basketball game, more often than not, we are all in the bleachers rooting him on.

One of the best family times for us occurs at day's end. Children are always anxious to stay up just a little bit longer. Many parents resist this, and no small amount of frowning and whining can result. We've been able to avoid this tussle with reading time. The entire family assembles in the living room where all of us take turns reading aloud. Sometimes it is out of the family Bible, but often, each family member brings a special story or passage from a book. It is fair to say that each of our children have learned to read in these sessions. But more importantly, the reading allows a special quiet time of kinship and security to be enjoyed by the entire family. The mind settles and is at rest. When the reading is concluded, the family evening prayer can be said. Afterward, sleep is seldom resisted. Perhaps, it is simply reverence for God that ushers the day to close with gentle reflection and contentment.

Family functions and family times go together. Unlike the "unreal" television drama or overstated news event, they create lasting memories of fun and work. And they create an atmosphere in which the qualities of self-control, patience, and understanding—those derived from the personal cardinal virtues discussed in later chapters—are easily nourished.

Law Is Not Morality

Television is a form of unreality. For a family, the law—if it is introduced within the family as the governing moral standard—can be as well. Let me explain.

Turning off the television, focusing on local news in the paper, and re-establishing (or maybe establishing for the first time) genuine family times and functions is a necessary first step to enhanced moral formation. Sometimes this step is impeded, however, by an argument like . . . well, it's not against school rules or the law to do something. For example, it may not be against the law for teenagers to hang around the mall all afternoon (or at least the vagrancy statutes aren't enforced strictly enough to stop it), so the argument goes, this time-wasting, trouble-inviting, mindless practice must be all right. So too movie theaters seldom exclude anyone from R or PG-13 rated movies, even as what may be shown under these labels may be highly damaging to a young person, or even adults.

Family Prescription

* Aspire to higher family standards than the law designates.

Parents should recognize the "it's not against the law" argument as simply a variant of "Dad or Mom, everybody is doing it," as in "everybody is going swimming after the prom" or "everyone is bringing shaving cream to soap up the school windows on the last day before summer vacation," etc. The response in our household to this line is: "Well, we are *not* raising everyone." What these arguments try to do is to substitute or re-introduce the lax or minimum standard of the crowd (often formed at the knee of the television stranger) in place of a family's more aspiring or proper one.

Now, this happens outside the family as well, but we may not recognize it as easily. This is the insidious confusion between law and morality. Thirty years ago, this wasn't much of a problem because, quite frankly, the law was favorable to families. Divorce was limited to occasions of serious fault. Illegitimacy was rare. Both were frowned upon. Abortion was a crime, as was sex outside marriage (fornication) or homosexual sodomy. I need not detail the changes in the law over the past three decades because they are painfully obvious and, in most cases, the opposite of prior law. All are antagonistic to the family and reasonable efforts to shape moral character.

Does the fact that divorce or abortion can now be readily obtained in the world external to your family make it right? Obviously not. But given the tremendous struggle and concentration on changing especially abortion *laws* in the Supreme Court and the Congress (the "fool's game" discussed in the previous chapter), we may forget that the most important thing is for each of us and our family members to act morally, not whether the law authorizes immoral behavior. The law cannot make that which is morally wrong, right. But neither will correcting an aberrant law correct our own personal character failings.

To make this point clearer, it is useful to state plainly the difference between morality and law. Morality governs all of human conduct. It's aim is the doing of good; and it relies upon the development of habits of virtue (temperance, prudence, courage, and so forth)—the kind of habits that really only families can instill. By contrast, law—as pointed out earlier—looks to the public order; it relies ultimately on force or coercion. Law cannot make one a better person or lead a better life. At best, it can create the conditions minimally necessary for worthy moral pursuits.

The Supreme Court itself has done much to confuse law and morality by taking cases for review that have no warrant in constitutional text or history. The Court has compounded the confusion by issuing opinions that read more like the musings of political philosophers than justices with the limited function of parsing the meaning of constitutional provisions and narrowly drawn statutes. For example, *Roe v. Wade* and every subsequent abortion decision purports, despite hollow judicial disclaimers, to settle when life begins; another case dealing with the withdrawal of medical treatment purports to determine life's end. Other cases assume to proclaim when it is "right" to exclude religion or to take race or gender into account.

Regrettably, the Court has not been alone in the disregard of the difference between law and morality. As John Courtney Murray, S.J. wrote over thirty years ago: There is a "constant shout: 'There ought to be a Law!' That is, whenever it appears that some good thing needs doing, or some evil thing needs to be done away with, the immediate cry is for the arm of the law."[7]

To overlook the limits of the law is to confuse law with the reality vital to family stability and well-being. No law can prevent, or fully rectify, the mishaps of life, be they car accidents or medical malpractice. No law can raise or educate our children or help them appreciate the immorality of abortion or sexual relations outside marriage. No law can ensure the fairness of every economic transaction or the "just" distribution of wages and property. When the law pretends to such fanciful objectives, as President Clinton would have it do in matters of health care, it raises unrealistic expectations and fails miserably.

Worse, when law is enlisted to do morality's work, that which is legal is by parity—or perhaps I should say "parody"—of reasoning thought to be moral. If it's not against the law, then the refrain continues, it must be all right. But, in *reality*, there is nothing "all right" about the taking of innocent life, be it before birth or at the option of Dr. Kevorkian. In the last chapter, it was said to be a "fool's game" to try to re-establish virtue through law or politics. The corollary stated here is that it is equally foolish for a family to accept the law as the definition of virtue. Any family that does so is organizing life around that which is artificial, rather than real.

Do not misunderstand. This is not a call for neutrality by individuals or families to the public side of moral questions. Nor is it

---

7   John Courtney Murray, *We Hold These Truths* (Kansas City, Mo.: Sheed & Ward, 1960).

an invitation to keep moral sentiments private. It is, however, to contend that the appeal to moral sentiments must occur first in home and church, where such sentiments can mold, rather than divide. With moral obligation better understood and accepted at home and religious base, members of family and religious congregation can thereafter make moral claims on the public square that are at once more genuine and explicit.

Family Prescription

   * **Assert family sovereignty; all families are not alike.**

It is perhaps revealing that the most noted chronicler of the culture war, James Davison Hunter, overstates the need for "a universal system of law and justice."[8] Uniformity of viewpoint is a false premise; it is not part of the intended constitutional design— and for good reason. America is a nation of separate sovereigns, most notably, the fifty states and thousands of municipal governments but our individual families as well. Each within its own scope of authority has a different conception of what ought and ought not be written into law. The original Constitution of the United States required "a universal system of law and justice" only where the national economy (interstate commerce, the issuance of money) or the national defense demanded it. Elsewhere, we are entitled to "equal justice under law," not identical laws. What's more, the call for uniform, national law overlooks the special "sovereignty" of the family. To take family life seriously, each family must undertake to direct children toward habits of virtue based on the mega-virtues of belief in God and knowable truth that are far in excess of the uniform or universal minimums of the federal law.

It is not entirely surprising that the reporters of culture war have been misled on this point. While the *intended* American structure was one of limited government and federalism, the last half-century of legal and political development has been in the contrary direction. The World Wars and the national economic Depression yielded a dominating, intrusive federal presence and legal and political positions that perhaps made sense as short-term responses to emergency but are untenable and in tension with any real desire to revive personal responsibility and virtue.

---

8   Hunter, *Before the Shooting Begins* (New York: Free Press, 1994), p. 18.

desire to return to the federalist constitutional structure, where
states and local governments are not mere vassals or sub-agencies
of the national government. Even the Supreme Court seems at-
tuned to this sentiment by hearing argument in a case that asks
bluntly: "Is there *no* limit to federal power?"[9] If realized, these
favorable federalist or decentralizing legal and political impulses
should help families distinguish the real from the artificial. After
all, that which is local and close-at-hand is better evaluated than
that at a distance.

But the family itself must aid this re-direction by re-asserting its
own sovereignty. Family sovereignty posits that the most accurate
view of life is gained from bottom-up, not top-down. It relies upon
the concept of *subsidiarity*, which holds that authority ought never
be arrogated to a higher level where it can be successfully exercised
below. Subsidiarity should not be confused with individualism or
radical autonomy. Quite the contrary, subsidiarity is an intellectual
bridge between individual, the individual family, and the common
good. It is the right to be let alone but only where such right is
bounded by the exercise of reasoned judgment and personal responsibility for oneself *and others* in the community. Subsidiarity is
also, in part, a religiously informed doctrine—most notably, out of
the Catholic tradition. It is ironic, therefore, that some American
Catholic bishops seemed to be "appalled" by the prospect of the
downsizing of the federal welfare presence by the post-1994 GOP
Congress. Had the reality of subsidiarity been perceived without
the artificially created national presence, a smaller federal government should have been warmly welcomed by these prelates as an
opportunity for churches and families to resume their legitimate
authority and resources.

In some ways, then, expecting the law or the courts to be our
moral guides is as risky as expecting good advice from the TV
stranger. Like the television, the law is not drawn to virtue but to
minimal or lower interests. TV and the law both appeal to the masses.
The standards within our families must appeal to our strengths,
not our weaknesses. They ought to call us to exercise our very best
judgment and behavior, and not assume the least acceptable.

The so-called culture war is launched on a faulty premise—that
moral growth within the family depends upon political or legal

9   *U.S. v. Lopez*, 2 F. 3d 1342 (5th Cir 1993), *cert. granted*, 114 S. Ct. 1536
      (1994). The Court in late April 1995 held that there is a limit, but it is
      still a bit hazy as to where that limit is.

ire war is launched on a faulty premise—that
the family depends upon political or legal
eyors of culture war bemoan the politicization
roups, and professional organizations and
them, but they ultimately decline to sever the
een politics and morality. As one writes: "The
the abandonment of politics. To imagine that
we could depoliticize these controversies at this point would be
sheer illusion."[10] We cannot, it is argued, "retreat into the realm of
private life." Instead, the reporters of culture war lamely pro-
nounce "democracy must be reinvented in every generation...." But
what this means is no more enlightening than the superficial
bumper-sticker positions that presently masquerade as national
debate.

Families need not retreat, so much as renew. If families turn off
the TV, refocus on local (rather than national issues), establish
family functions, and set high moral standards independent of
what other's may be doing or what the law allows, and then
proclaim those standards in their own lives, a culture war is avoid-
able.

But avoiding a culture war is itself a minimalist objective. What
American families are really after is leading a life of goodness—
where children are well-behaved and desire to learn and progress
through the various stages of physical, mental, and spiritual
growth; where parents' love for each other can survive difficulty
and argument; where neighbors and co-workers respect and help
each other; where public order is maintained; where men and
women can freely worship. If American families are to pursue this
life of goodness, it will not be by dint of government program or
legal pronouncement, it will be by a genuine family embrace of the
necessary beliefs that make a life of virtue and merit and goodness
possible. This requires a re-orientation of family philosophy toward the mega-and personal virtues described next.

---

10   Hunter, *Before the Shooting Begins*, pp. 242–43.

Chapter 4
Mega-Virtue No. 1—
Belief in God

BELIEF IN GOD IS VITAL to cultural virtue; for many of us, it is indispensable to personal virtue as well.

Controversial? Perhaps, or so it may seem in the shadow of the artificial world of the television stranger where there is a regular denial of the significance of God to our well-being. In real life, however, Dwight Eisenhower—the last U. S. President before the age of denial and skepticism—summed matters up well: "recognition of the Supreme Being is the first, the most basic, expression of Americanism. Without God, there could be no American form of Government, no American way of life."[1] Apparently, Americans still agree, as over 95 percent of Americans say they believe in God or a universal spirit.[2] Nevertheless, to the modern ear, President Eisenhower's comment and even the high percentage of believers reflected in contemporary polling data seem artificially overstated, even contrived. But why?

It has become commonplace for politicians to speak reverently of God; that is, so long as they are at a prayer breakfast. This is what is known in the trade as America's "civil religion," or as one writer put it, "faintly Protestant platitudes which reaffirm the religious base of American culture despite being largely void of theological significance."[3] Elsewhere, God's significance to the public debate not only goes largely unaffirmed, but also is—pursuant to Supreme

---

1   Will Herberg, *Protestant-Catholic-Jew* (New York: Anchor Books, 1960), p. 258 (quoting Eisenhower).

2   Jeffrey L. Sheler, "Spiritual America," *U.S. News & World Report* (April 4, 1994), p. 48.

3   Frederick M. Gedicks, "The Religious, the Secular, and the Anti-thetical," 20 *Capital Univ. L. Rev.* 113, 122 (1991).

Court opinion—deliberately excluded. But more worrisome than either the shallowness of political rhetoric or the incoherence of judicial opinion is that the genuine acknowledgment of belief in God can be equally limited or only superficial in our own lives and that of our family. As Stephen Carter describes in his challenging book, *The Culture of Disbelief*: "[W]e often seem most comfortable with people whose religions consist of nothing but a few private sessions of worship and prayer, but who are too secularized to let their faiths influence the rest of the week. This attitude exerts pressure to treat religion as a hobby . . . ."[4]

Belief in God Must Have Personal Significance for the Family

God is not a hobby. But how does one make an appealing case for belief in God? Historical, even presidential, citation seems hardly up to the task, though such could be legion from Washington to Clinton. No, if the case for God is to be successful, God's significance must be more personally understood. What is that significance? *Without God, our individual human lives, and all of human existence including family life, is without objective purpose.*

Stop, for a moment, and think about that statement. It is a sizeable claim, and one that will be resisted by nonbelievers and even many casual believers. Yet, the significance of God's revealed teaching is everywhere. God instructs each of us to honor parents and to be faithful to our spouse. When we fail to do so, as when we understate the value of the marriage commitment, the awful results are obvious as they have been over the past thirty years: "a 419% increase in illegitimate births; a quadrupling in divorce rates; a tripling of the percentage of children living in single-parent homes; more than a 200% increase in the teenage suicide rate; and a drop of almost 80 points in SAT scores."[5] When we cheapen respect for life by leaving the unborn unprotected or allow the elderly to languish without emotional support through the pain of age or permit violence to dominate television and movie production all contrary to God's clear injunction "not to kill," a 560 percent increase in violent crime over the past three decades should not come as a surprise.

---

4   Stephen L. Carter, *The Culture of Disbelief* (New York: Basic Books, 1993), p. 29.

5   William J. Bennett, "Quantifying America's Decline," *Wall Street Journal* (March 15, 1993), p. A10.

30 CEASE-FIRE ON THE FAMILY

Confronting the Moral Skeptic in Us and Others

But the skeptic—the modern American "policy wonk"—will say, "What has this to do with God?" If the crime rate is high, build more prisons and stiffen penalties. If marriages fail to last, eliminate no-fault divorce. If schools are failing to teach, spend more money on them or create a structure of public-private competition. In themselves, each of these responses may contain, in appropriate contexts, helpful prescriptions for what ails us. But each of these policy treatments also assume a recognition of illness, of dysfunction. By what standard is dysfunction measured? In other words, what insures that the "killing" of a human person will be actually understood as wrong (a point apparently lost on the Menendez jury); that single-parenthood, while tragically unavoidable because of death, nevertheless should not be extolled as just another living arrangement (a matter of some dispute between former Vice-President Quayle and "Murphy Brown")? For many, only belief in God—as a transcendent authority—can supply this standard reliably.

The skeptic still resists. I don't need God, he says, to know that murder is off-limits, and my kids know better than to get pregnant outside of marriage. Perhaps, but the statistics say otherwise. But, says the skeptic, I am not a statistic, my family is different. There is the chance of this. It is possible, albeit difficult, to discover some truth, unaided even by God, as it were. The difficulty is, of course, that our reasoning is not perfect. And even if we are reluctant to admit this shortcoming about ourselves, we readily ascribe imperfection to others. Here the skeptic may—if he is honest—at least hesitate. He can hear himself saying how foolish his neighbor is to let his daughter stay out all night after the prom or how ridiculous it is for the government to subsidize illegitimate births through its welfare programs as is obvious by the disturbing fact that 71 percent of all new welfare cases are headed by never-married mothers.[6]

From God Comes Family and Social Order

Belief in the existence of God calibrates the moral compass. It is with this compass for determining right from wrong that Americans interact within families and take actions that affect others.

---

6 Ben Wattenberg, "Circle of Welfare Must Be Cut," *Human Events* (July 24, 1993), p. 7, citing the Congressional Research Service.

Accepting God supplies what Tocqueville called the "dogmatic beliefs" that underlie the formation of community. He writes: "[I]t can never happen that there are no dogmatic beliefs, that is to say, opinions which men take on trust without discussion. If each man undertook to make up his mind about everything himself and to pursue truth only along roads that he himself had cleared, it is unlikely that any large number of people would ever succeed in agreeing on any common belief."[7]

The American Revolution was about preserving the dogmatic belief in the existence of God as part of the underlying philosophy of the nation, even as the founders resisted religious coercion and denominational preference. More on this shortly, but it would be the most profound error to conclude that religious tolerance sprung from indifference to the moral truths associated with a belief in God. Premised upon "self-evident" propositions of the good derived from the "Laws of Nature and Nature's God" in the Declaration of Independence, the ancient ideas of what is good or just were intended to motivate or guide our behavior in private, but especially from the standpoint of social order, in public. Our founders knew that these ideas are important to the creation and preservation of the community as a whole. If our skeptic happens upon moral truth by his own wits, fine. But the skeptic has no protection from others, either less willing or able, to discern the moral precepts supplied so clearly and simply by God.

Without the acknowledgment of God's existence generally, the family and the larger community fails to take form, and it is not likely to be oriented toward the accomplishment of any real good. We are guided not by common, accepted belief, but by isolated interests or wants. These "interests" are often far less positive than any of God's instruction. What's more, these narrow interests often arise out of envy or selfishness. Thus, within the family, husbands and wives war over who provides more household support than the other or whose turn it is to have "time at the sports club" or "with the girls at the mall." Children too seem to mount a regular campaign of "gimme," without a thought to "much-obliged." Meanwhile, outside the family, homosexuals war with heterosexuals; women against men; women at work against women at home; African-American against white; city dweller versus suburbanite.

---

7   Alexis de Tocqueville, *Democracy in America*, trans. George Lawrence (Chicago: Encylopedia Britannica, Inc., 1991), p. 229–30.

The 1992 election was ostensibly fought over protecting the middle class from everyone else. The rich would be taxed because, well, simply because they were rich. Envy had become campaign slogan and policy justification. Soo too, the 1994 mid-term elections seem less a return to personal and cultural virtue than an opposing response in-kind.

Belief in God—More Meaningful than a Mercedes

But even if we have now convinced the skeptic that belief in the existence of God knits together the American family and community in ways that intuition or self-interest cannot, is it possible to convince him that it is ultimately only belief in God which supplies meaning and coherence in *his* own life? This will be uphill. It is part of our nature as human beings to seek such comfort or well-being as earth can supply. To seek material things. And since we tend to devote so much of life to the pursuit of these comforts, we can hear ourselves saying: If only I had a newer car or an extra bedroom or the latest kitchen appliance.

Now, there is nothing wrong with having a nice home or auto, perhaps even a Mercedes (although I am told they are quite costly to service—or at least this is what I tell myself as I drive around in what my "car-crazy" 16-year-old tells me is much less). Belief in God does not require denial of this inclination. If it did, "sooner or later one may be sure that men's souls would slip through [and] plunge headlong into the delights of purely material and immediate satisfactions."[8]

Yet, material and earthly rewards do distract every one of us from examining our ultimate end. Were it genuinely possible for our skeptic—despite his intelligence or wealth—to grasp some highly unfortunate circumstance such as being diagnosed with untreatable cancer, the significance of belief in God would likely be more apparent. When confronted with death, what does it matter if one has a Mercedes or a Mazda or a large or small house or a competitor is getting the edge in the market?

More Meaningful Even than Our Family Role

If it is impossible for us to imagine facing death, other questions might be asked: for example, who really cares about what authority

---

8   Tocqueville, *supra* at 238.

we exercise over others or where we work or what income we make? Our spouses? Our children? Yes, they care out of a certain material dependency, but if we were disabled from gainful employment, would that render us unimportant, purposeless, or expendable to them? We are apt to say no in the hope that our families would still love us for whom, not what, we are. But what accounts for this love? What prevents them from sending us away as a useless appendage in the back of Dr. Kevorkian's death wagon?

It might be thought that the mere status of being father, mother, grandparent, or sibling is enough explanation. Here we would be closer to the truth, but we would still be forced to explain why this status was important. Putting this into words is more difficult than may be thought. Yet, it is necessary.

So what do we say? We might say that we revere mother, for example, because she gave us life. Life being essential to all else that follows, a parent is therefore entitled to respect. But what if the life that follows is full of hardship or pain? Do we then treat mother with disrespect? File a law suit against her for a wrongful life? Any child who contemplated this would rightly be chastised as ungrateful or worse. But why?

More Meaningful than Philosophy and Science

The best philosophical minds have considered such questions throughout history. They have not had much success in supplying answers. "[F]or all their efforts," Tocqueville again writes, "they have done no more than discover a small number of contradictory ideas on which the mind of man has been carelessly tossed for thousands of years without ever firmly grasping the truth or even finding mistakes that are new."[9] The mind of man is simply not up to the task of explaining our ultimate purpose, when our origin is traced, not to an intelligent purposeful God, but nothing. Yet, this is all that modern philosophy can offer.

The scientific explanation for life's purpose is also wanting. Indeed, the current fashion in science attempts to explain all life in terms of the laws of physics (gravity, electromagnetic, weak and strong nuclear forces) and the chemistry of lifeless matter (DNA) traceable in some as-yet-unidentified manner to an unexplained "Big Bang," in which a symmetry of these forces may have existed. The federal government spent over $8 billion on a supercollider

---

9   Tocqueville, *supra* at 235.

that was supposed to confirm a minor step in the Big Bang theory. The supercollider yielded no such confirmation, but it is hard to see how even if it had, how that would have explained the love between mother and child—even one born into hardship and poverty—or the respect we give to others generally.

Please understand, this is not to denigrate scientific inquiry. However, it does suggest that we should be wary of trying to base our family's pursuit of virtue, or our individual lives, on theories that demand we accept "an impersonal universe that exists for no purpose."[10] One of the most prominent scientists in the "Big Bang" effort is candid about this desire to displace God, in the assumption that any retained theism is nothing more than a rejection of rational thought.[11] Yet, how can this be so, when all that science will reveal—if it ever does reveal this—is the method by which life originated, not *why* it did. And it is only in the why of life that answers of what to value and whom to respect can be found. The why of life can only be supplied by someone greater than life itself.

Second-Best (but Still Pretty Good) Reasons for Belief in God

If the skeptic remains unpersuaded, the best case for belief in God may have to be a second-best, but still persuasive, look at the consequences of its absence. The statistics of cultural decline during the past thirty years recited earlier parallel the legal exclusion of God from the public square. And when God's values do not guide, any value and all values, as contradictory or hurtful as they may be, have free reign and equal claim to allegiance. As the existentialist Jean Paul Sartre wrote: "If I have done away with God the Father, someone is needed to invent values . . . life has no meaning [then in itself] . . . it is up to you to give it meaning, and value is nothing but the meaning that you choose."[12]

The first casualty of God's denial is the absence of civil order, virtue—the absence of culture. If nothing governs our relationship with each other but that which we choose, the strong or the clever

---

10   Phillip E. Johnson, "Science without God," *Wall Street Journal* (May 10, 1993), p. A10.

11   See Steven Weinberg, *Dreams of a Final Theory* (New York: Pantheon Books, 1992).

12   Jean Paul Sartre, *Existentialism*, trans. Bernard Frechtman (New York: Philosophical Society, 1947), p. 58.

or the mob will have their way with us. If they have the weaponry, why shouldn't Serbs kill Croats or Germans, Jews or Tutsis, Hutus? True, civil order may from time to time be premised upon "social contract" or "consent," but if we tire of the arrangement—if, in Sartre's phraseology, we choose to give significance to new values of our choosing—the contract can be breached, the constitution amended.

Along with civil order, the personal order of our lives—especially our family lives—similarly destruct. Unlike animals, men and women do not act on instinct. Rather, there is action linked to reason, purpose. But again, something must supply this purpose. If it is not God, then what? Over fifty years ago, a commentator on the American scene wrote: "Could anything replace [God] but 'Democracy' made into an object of worship, or business, or success?" This writer speculated then that "Nobody knew; nobody knows, yet."[13] In this, he was too tentative. The error of thinking that man or any of his human idols or political structures can replace God is apparent from the failure of every frail or transient substitute for God to satisfy. What's more, today, we know more than ever that political majorities do not necessarily act with justice. In the insightful words of the late Russell Kirk:

> [a]ll the aspects of any civilization arise out of a people's religion: its politics, its economics, its arts, its sciences, even its simple crafts are the by-products of religious insights.... For until human beings are tied together by some common faith, and share certain moral principles, they prey upon one another.... At the very heart of every culture is a body of ethics, of distinctions between good and evil; and in the beginning at least, those distinctions are founded upon the authority of revealed religion. Not until a people have come to share religious belief are they able to work together satisfactorily, or even to make sense of the world in which they find themselves.[14]

Belief in God Is Not a Denial of Religious Freedom

In the claim that belief in God is a necessary part of restoring

13   Denis W. Brogan, *The American Character* (New York: Alfred A. Knopf, 1944), p. 102.

14   Russell Kirk, *The Roots of the American Order* 3d ed. (Washington, D.C.: Regnery Gateway, 1991), p. 14.

cultural virtue in America, it will be carefully observed that no case is made for a particular religious sect. The American tradition is the product of numerous religious influences, and the founders had great distaste for coerced religious belief or practice.

The diversity of religious practice that underlies belief in God as it is discussed here contributes many individual nuances to the American character. From the Hebrew tradition, we gain an understanding of man's sinfulness and imperfection and the importance of God's guidance. John Calvin and the Puritans took the law of the Hebrews, including the Ten Commandments and the books of Leviticus and Deuteronomy, and transplanted them to New England soil. What blossomed was an American democracy that has been "a highly moral adventure."[15] Calvinist thought, reflected in Anglican, Presbyterian, and Baptist teaching, for example, yielded in the American landscape "the contract and all its corollaries; the higher law as something more than a 'brooding omnipresence in the sky'; the concept of the competent and responsible individual; certain key ingredients of economic individualism; the insistence on a citizenry educated to understand its rights and duties; and the middle-class virtues, that high plateau of moral stability on which, so Americans believe, successful democracy must always build."[16] The Catholic tradition of St. Thomas Aquinas became the wellspring for the English common law and equity, by way of the Magna Carta and influential legal treatises by Blackstone and others that directly shaped the minds of the founding generation. It was Blackstone, it will be remembered, who wrote that "the law of nature being coequal with mankind and dictated by God himself, is of course superior in obligation to any other. It is binding over all the globe, and all countries, and at all times; no human laws are of any validity if contrary to this; . . ."[17]

Belief in God Requires a Recognition of Law's Limits

Belief in God is thus nondenominational or, more precisely, multi-denominational. What the philosophical import of belief in

---

15   Clinton Rossiter, *Seedtime of the Republic: The Origin of the American Tradition of Political Liberty* (New York: Harcourt, Brace & Co., 1953), p. 55.

16   Id.

17   William Blackstone, *Commentaries on the Laws of England* (originally published 1765; Chicago: University of Chicago Press, 1979), p. 41.

God means is this: that transcendent authority imposes duty; that this duty relates to both the spiritual and temporal worlds, and thus, relates to both what is due God and others here on earth; and that the precise duties that are imposed advance public order by restraining human willfulness, including any inclination to do harm to oneself or others, but leave unrestrained political, scientific, or personal inquiry. Because the multi-denominational belief in God does not impose any specific religious creed, there is an implied reciprocal understanding that the democratic process will not command observance of any law directly contrary to the core articles of faith of any specific denomination, except those absolutely essential to public order. As discussed earlier, it is important to recognize the fundamental difference between the law and morality.

Modern controversies over abortion and homosexuality may suggest that this last point has not been faithfully observed. In fact, however, despite profound disagreements over these issues, the democratic process (including the Supreme Court) has yet to command by and large that anyone personally engage in or condone the practice of abortion or homosexuality. That would clearly be improper. Thus, conscientious-objection laws do (and as a matter of morality must) give believers, in the carrying out of their private or professional duties—for example, doctors and health care personnel in hospitals—an opportunity to withdraw without penalty from the taking of any action against life. *Most importantly*, Biblical and church teaching can and should be followed within the family and church community, even as the law is antagonistic.

But the complaint of many religious adherents goes beyond such circumstances to include the failure of the law to align itself fully with Biblical or other church teaching, or in other words, the failure for law and morality to coincide. This is a significant complaint, especially as Biblical or church teaching supporting the sanctity of unborn life or decrying homosexual liaisons as a spiritual and physical disorder is an accurate reflection of human nature. What's more, the nonalignment of law and morality in these grave instances results in serious moral conflict for believers occupying public position. Recognizing this, an important Catholic encyclical recently instructed that when it is not possible to overturn or completely abrogate, for example, a law directly antagonistic to life, "an elected official whose absolute personal opposition . . . is well known could licitly support proposals aimed at limiting the harm done by such a law and at lessening its negative consequences at the level of general opinion and public morality. This does not in fact represent an illicit cooperation with an unjust law, but rather a legitimate and proper attempt to limit its evil aspects."[18]

Unfortunately, the law has, at times, commanded what belief in God forbids. For example, laws or judicial decisions that authorize minor daughters to obtain an abortion without parental consent through a so-called "judicial bypass" undermine the superior authority of parents. So too one must include President Clinton's directives that mandate that all taxpayers subsidize abortion counseling or advocacy and, even worse, the actual performance of abortions with Medicaid funding. While few in number, the examples are tragic, and do much to explain the increasing levels of civil disobedience. They, of course, never justify violence. Nonetheless, if lawmakers are serious about the restoration of cultural virtue, any law that mandates that individuals or families act contrary to their religious beliefs without a compelling justification tied to the preservation of public order must be considered highly suspect and, in all likelihood, invalid.

Belief in God Is Not Unconstitutional

Some families may be reluctant to wholeheartedly acknowledge belief in God as part of their pursuit of virtue for fear that this would make them outcasts in their own country. This reluctance is so often traced to the confusing, and frequently hostile, treatment religion has received in the Supreme Court in the past thirty years that stopping here for a closer look at the Constitution and its history is warranted.

The importance of belief in God to the founders of America is perhaps best revealed by the fact that several states necessary for the successful ratification of the Constitution did so only on condition that the Constitution would be amended to guarantee religious freedom. What resulted was the First Amendment: "Congress shall make no law respecting an establishment of religion, or prohibiting the free exercise thereof; . . ." *Two* provisions—no established church and the freedom to exercise the denominational belief or practice of one's choice—*one* common objective: religious free-

---

18   John Paul II, "The Gospel of Life," (Evangelium Vitae), *Origins*, Vol. 24, No. 42, (April 6, 1995), para. 73.

dom. The government may neither *pre*scribe religious faith, nor *pro*scribe it.

It is historically understandable why the founders would insist on this religious protection. Thomas Jefferson's notes reflect how the nation was settled by immigrants fleeing the coercion and persecution of the laws of England demanding support of the established Anglican Church. Regretfully, some who fled to the new nation then adopted "equal intolerance" in the colonies. For example, some colonies and early states had established churches, where everyone—even religious dissenters—were required to pay taxes to the favored church, worship at official church services or be subject to penalty, submit to religious tests and oaths in order to hold office or vote, and, on pain of being banished from the colony, subscribe to particular religious creeds.[19]

To counter this coercion, Jefferson drafted an Act for Establishing Religious Freedom in Virginia, which provided that "no man shall be compelled to frequent or support any religious worship, place, or ministry whatsoever, . . ; but that all men shall be free to profess, and by argument to maintain, their opinion in matters of religion, . . ."[20] It is important to understand what this Act does: It prohibits religious compulsion *in order to guarantee* the freedom to profess religion. It is not freedom *from* religion but freedom to *embrace* religion.

The final wording of the first amendment to the Constitution reflects this perspective. The government may not "make law" establishing a religion. By definition, a law involves a binding obligation under threat of compulsion. Until 1962, the nation was faithful to this understanding. Founded on an appeal "to the Supreme Judge of the world," virtually every president has invoked God's blessings on the undertakings of the United States. George Washington noted how "it would be peculiarly improper to omit in [his] first official act [his] fervent supplications to that Almighty Being who rules over the universe. . . ."[21] The Congress opens its

---

19   Joseph Brady, *Confusion Twice Confounded: The First Amendment and the Supreme Court* (South Orange, N.J.: Seton Hall University Press, 1954), pp. 6–7.

20   An Act for Establishing Religious Freedom (Virginia, 1785),in Philip Kurland and Ralph Lerner, eds., *The Founders' Constitution*, 5 (Chicago: University of Chicago Press, 1987), p. 85.

21   George Washington, First Inaugural Address, April 30, 1789.

sessions with prayer, then and now. To this day, Supreme Court
sessions begin with the invocation: "God save the United States and
this Honorable Court."

Yet, it is the Supreme Court that has stricken belief in God from
the day-to-day experience of modern America. In *Engel v. Vitale*
(1962),[22] the Court was confronted with a challenge to state-man-
dated prayer in a school classroom. The Court held that the prayer
violated the First Amendment, even though it was, as one of the
dissenting justices noted, no different from the reference to God
made by the Court itself. However, unlike sessions of the Supreme
Court, students are mandated to attend school, and in this, there
may be found improper compulsion when the school day starts
with the words, "Let us pray" in reference to a particular religious
source. This is a legitimate concern. No school child should be
coerced into praying, contrary to his family's faith, to Allah rather
than Christ or to read the Koran rather than the Bible. But, by the
same token, every school child should be able to learn the religious
traditions of his family and its relationship to leading a good life
and to the preparation for life's work. The imposed uniformity of
the public school when juxtaposed against the multi-denominational nature of the American population appears to make genuine
religious practice and instruction in that public setting practically
impossible.

For this reason, the government—at least for believers—is disabled from being a supplier of education. How can a child be truly
educated toward virtue if a primary, or mega-virtue (belief in God)
must be excluded? To ask the question is to answer it. In the context
of the narrow issues of litigated cases, the larger issue of government disability in matters of education for virtue has been either
left unaddressed or obscured by the legalism of constitutional
doctrine. In this regard, it has yet to be fully realized by believing
parents that the Court's declaration of neutrality between religion
and no religion is the government's confession of inability to act as
moral educator.

The Court's exclusionary position dressed in language of neutrality has been unwisely extended beyond the public school.
Crosses in public parks, nativity scenes on courthouse steps, menorahs in squares are banished unless they can be hidden among
secular symbols. A federal court has invalidated the closure of

22   370 U.S. 421 (1962).

government offices on Good Friday. Accepting that courts may be rightly perplexed by how teacher directions to pray can be reconciled with a coercive mandate to attend public school hardly explains the banishment of all religious reference not just in schools but in public generally. No religious belief or practice is compelled, for example, by having a day off. Nonetheless, by judicial decree, a "nation under God"—in its multi-denominational sense—has been transformed into a nation noncommittal toward God.

Proclaiming the Constitution to be strictly neutral between religion and no religion, of course, did not make it so. With religion off-limits, everything that was not God became, in the eyes of the law, superior to God. And so the First Amendment intended to secure in law a cultural context that was congenial to the mega-virtue of belief in God came to be used as a vehicle to exclude God and religion. The intended protection against coercion became itself an instrument of coercion and expulsion of God.

The irony, if not illogic, of the Court's handiwork troubles those trained or untrained in the law alike, but the consequences are clear. A nation founded confidently in the expression that "we hold these truths" now timorously and aimlessly recites, "we are neutral as to truth." Religious symbols—be they nativity scenes, menorahs, or portraits of religious figures—are banned from public buildings and squares. No substantive discussion of God's moral instruction can take place in public school, as even the Ten Commandments may not be posted. A school-planned invocation or benediction at a public school assembly is forbidden. Court's accept the recital of the pledge of allegiance only because the words "one nation under God" have been drained of all meaning. All of this is made much worse by the fact that many American families have—practically and financially—no escape from the public schools (a matter addressed in a later chapter).

The Resuscitation of Belief in God Depends on the American Family

Were the Rev. Martin Luther King, Jr., alive, the law as interpreted by the Supreme Court would likely deny him the ability to repeat his 1961 commencement address at a public school. It will be recalled that in this emotion-filled address, Dr. King yearned for "the day when all of God's children, black men and white men, Jews and Gentiles, Catholics and Protestants, will be able to join hands and sing in the words of the old Negro spiritual, "Free at last! Free at last! Thank God Almighty, we are free at last!" How diminished the world would be if those words had not been expressed.

But God's plan gave us Martin's words. And again, importantly, the law is not morality. The hopeful words of Martin Luther King, Jr., *can* be uttered in every American home and church. Regardless of Supreme Court misinterpretation, it is in those homes and churches where the freedom Dr. King yearned for either will be nourished or forfeited.

America's freedom is dependent upon social order and the personal ordering of the soul within the American family. It is here where belief in God matters most.

Chapter 5
Mega-Virtue No. 2—
A Knowable Truth

THE AMERICAN FAMILY, and through it, the American nation, cannot long survive without some basic, fundamental differentiation between truth and falsity.

The Declaration of Independence proclaims: "We hold these truths to be self-evident . . . ." But the understanding of the Declaration has been overtaken since the 1960s by an insidious claim of moral skepticism or relativism. As one writer puts it, "[A]ll moral judgments are *nothing but* expressions of preference, expressions of attitude or feeling, . . ."[1] You say abortion is murder; another says it is a matter of free choice. Others find sexual relations outside of marriage to be antagonistic to the family and the well-being of children, only to be opposed by unmarried couples who insist that these people mind their own business. The disagreements have become so profound, it is claimed that "[i]n much public debate in America there is no longer clear distinction between human and animal, male and female, word and image, war and peace, invasion and liberation, law and violence, reason and madness, civilized and primitive, knowledge and ignorance, doctor and patient, citizenship and tribalism, persuasion and propaganda, art and pornography, reporting and fiction, character and instincts."[2]

One consequence of such radical disagreement over seemingly incommensurate values is: intellectual gridlock—that is, interminable discussion raising blood pressure, yet, settling nothing. Another consequence is moral aimlessness and indifference with the resulting cultural decline. The point of this chapter, in keeping with

---

1   Alisdair MacIntyre, *After Virtue*, 2d ed. (Notre Dame, Ind.: University of Notre Dame Press, 1984), p. 12 (taking issue with this view).

2   Os Guinness, *The American Hour* (New York: Free Press, 1993), p. 30.

the larger purpose of the book, is to say: enough already. It is to refresh modern memory of how, as American families, we can end intellectual gridlock and the accompanying paralysis and antagonism. How, in short, the culture war can be ended—not with rancor and force, or with moral default, but with a renewed understanding of freedom in a context of responsibility.

True or False—What Are the facts?

The first step is to explore what is wrong with the moral skepticism of the age, and to put it into some realistic perspective. How many of us, after all, assert that there is *no* knowable truth, that we are completely unsure of what is true and what is false? As a practical matter, few would hold such a belief. Take a simple example. You go to the car dealer to buy a new car. The dealer takes you out to the lot and points out a rusted heap of metal suggesting that this is the latest model from Tokyo (or, Lee Iaccocca help us) Detroit. Do you for a minute believe him? No! You say quite confidently that the dealer is being deceptive, and in making this statement you affirm that what is true can be separated from that which is not. Truth, as one great American thinker has put it, consists simply in "agreement or correspondence between mind and reality."[3]

But, you say, this is too simple. The cultural skirmishing that is occurring over the legitimacy of cohabitation or abortion or homosexuality relates to *opinion*, not fact. In other words, while it may be possible for all to agree that the rusty heap is not a new convertible, there is no possibility for proving in the same fashion that abortion or lesbianism is wrong or right. The moral relativist would claim in this that it is a mistake to believe that there is a moral reality against which opinions can be measured or evaluated.

Philosophers schooled in the classics have always had a clever, but ultimately unsatisfying, way of answering this type of critic of objective standards or a knowable truth. They simply point out that the critic or skeptic has contradicted himself. When the skeptic claims that it is a *mistake* to believe in a moral reality, he admits what his statement ostensibly denies, namely, that there is a standard by which an argument can be judged to be correct (true) or mistaken (false).

---

3   Mortimer J. Adler, *Six Great Ideas* (New York: Macmillan, 1981), p. 34.

The reason the clever philosophical response is not fully satisfying is that the skeptic is likely to persist, saying, So what if I contradicted myself; you still can't prove me wrong. It might be responded that those who are willingly contradictory are irrational or, at best, unreasonable. Since it is impossible to reach agreement with irrational and unreasonable people, we may be tempted to just disregard the skeptic. But doing so would be a weak defense of the truth needed to strengthen the American family in its pursuit of virtue.

True or False—Is It More than Opinion?

Contradictory or not, the skeptic has raised a troubling issue: How do we prove that a statement of opinion is true or false? Again, with statements of fact, this is relatively straightforward. A factual statement is either true or false in itself, regardless of the opinion that a person has about the fact's truth or falsity. I may claim that the Cubs won the World Series in 1994, but the falsity of that statement can be demonstrated by a look at the records which reveals a baseball strike and the absence of any Series play. Moreover, the false nature of my assertion remains false, even if hoards of championship-starved Chicagoans support my claim. But what of the moral statement of opinion—the statement that declares that a certain behavior is good and another evil? Can that also be checked in the "records"? Mega-virtue No. 2—a knowable truth—answers in the affirmative.

Family Prescription

* **Instruct your family based upon the assumption that moral reality exists, that there is objective moral truth.**

The only way to get on well in life is to come to grips with reality. With regard to the reality of our economic or physical condition, we remind ourselves of this with the expression not to keep "hitting a brick wall." For example, my eyesight is far from 20/20. To proceed on the assumption that I have the eyesight needed for an airline pilot would be to put myself and others in serious jeopardy. Similarly, a quick look at the savings account reminds me that I need to watch the family budget carefully so that tuition bills, car repairs,and the like can be met. On the positive side, the physical and economic reality of life invites me to certain activities. Thus, I have had sufficient talent to master a word-processor and finish various educational pursuits. These attainments direct me toward things that I can really—that is, in reality—do (for example, teach and write). And please don't say you have doubts about the latter and ask your bookstore for a refund!

Morality is no different. It is both a limit (like the brick wall) and an invitation (as in going through the door in the brick wall). If we are in a healthy moral condition, we will be able to accomplish more good—in the sense of advancing our own individual natures consistently with that of family members and the community—than if we let our moral condition deteriorate. To maintain physical condition, we know—all too painfully—that we must exercise in relation to the reality of our physical endowments. To enhance economic condition, we must work, save, and invest in light of existing economic conditions—the reality of the market. Moral condition is much the same. Moral capacity is enhanced by training and exercise in relation to cardinal virtues, such as prudence or courage (see later chapters on this), which take meaning from the reality of human nature—that is, what a human person needs (as opposed to merely wants) and what motivates a person to his or her highest aspirations.

As the family seeks to help its individual members act more in line with moral reality, a certain caution must be observed, namely, while objective moral—as well as factual—truth exists as a separate reality, our individual judgments about that truth may be mistaken or only partially informed. This may be because of lack of information, an undeveloped ability to think or reason, or the inability of the mind to comprehend reality.

If we ask ourselves and our families to make decisions based on insufficient information, we are being imprudent, and we will suffer for it. I once bought a family van in its very first model year against the sage advice of my dear father and consumer magazines that similarly advised against being the first consumer in line for a new mechanical product. Why such advice? Because it is only in that first model year that a car or van's performance can be assessed under actual driving conditions (that is, reality). I went ahead without this information, and, yes, wouldn't you know it, I was a pedestrian for some weeks.

Lack of information is usually overcome with inquiry and patience. An inability to reason or perceive reality is also overcome with similar effort, age, and formal education unless some mental or physical disease interferes. For example, a mental illness such as paranoia blocks perception of reality, even as the reasoning process continues. As one writer put it, "[t]he paranoid's mind is like a fast ship speeding along a fog-bound coastline without any navigational equipment. The engines may be running well, and the steering gear may be in excellent order, but the captain has no idea where she is going, and the ship will surely run on the rocks."[4] Few American families will run aground because of paranoia, thankfully; rather, the greater danger is that moral reality will be known and ignored. However, where a family member is genuinely in doubt over the contour of moral reality, the logical course is to remain as fair-minded as possible, seeking counsel from elders in the family and one's church.

For believers, falling back on the first mega-virtue, belief in God, will indeed be of tremendous assistance. God has not hidden truth from us, even as our human imperfection limits our vision of it. To the contrary, the Ten Commandments is a remarkably clear statement of moral reality. Does this mean that a nonbeliever has no access to truth? No. An absence or weakness in faith dims knowledge of the truth, but it does not obliterate it. Believer and nonbeliever are created in God's image (whether they willingly admit it or not), and therefore, every person's reason or intelligence is part of His image and, in that, linked to the source of truth.

As a practical matter, in times of doubt and uncertainty, it is very important for families to confront moral doubt squarely and not deny or ignore it. Families must work through such doubts with their children, reasoning in light of what the family already knows and exercising a presumption in favor of courses of action that the family sincerely believes will advance the human nature of the family member concerned and harm no one else's. Most importantly, families must always remember that *uncertainty over truth's content or its application, DOES NOT mean that truth does not exist.*

Family Checklist in the Event of Moral Doubt

1. Would the course of action being considered make the best, or at least constructive, use of talent and ability?
2. Would the course of action being considered be pursued even if it would not be recognized or rewarded in any way by others?

---

4   Philip E. Johnson, "Some Thoughts About Natural Law," 75 *Calif. L.Rev.* 217, 218 (1987).

3. Would the course of action being considered be of tangible good to, or relieve a misfortune of, someone else?
4. Is the course of action being considered respectful of the religious tradition of the family?
5. Is the course of action being considered one that would be recommended without hesitation for the person in the world you most care for?

To be sure, the checklist is not exhaustive. But if an affirmative answer can be given to each question, it is very likely that the proposed course of action of the family member will coincide with moral reality and, thus, promote the doing of good. The message is clear: Uncertainty or doubt should not lead any member of the family—whether strong or weak in faith—to moral relativism, or anything goes. Nor should it lead to a forfeiture of standard setting to the lawyers or politicians. Indeed, the presence of doubt or dispute should signal, if those men and women in the government are capable of exercising self-restraint, that this is a place where the law ought not be quick to impose a uniform rule. And as will be discussed in the next chapter, insofar as the public school is the "government school"—a mere extension of the state rather than the family and the family's faith—it too cannot be expected to be a reliable or apt source for alleviating moral doubt. To think that a public school with a uniform ideology and state-directed curriculum, or that law or government directive, can supply an answer in these doubt-laden cases is to invite to heightened social tension and re-kindling of cultural hostility. On a personal or family level, it is an ill-advised re-entry into the fool's game.

In moral questions as in matters of physical or economic activity, there is always the chance of error. (Just ask me sometime about the oil and gas limited partnership I bought once). Mistakes will be made. My father says that's why they put erasers on pencils. But to err is not to deny that there is a source of moral truth even in so-called matters of opinion. And, as briefly discussed below, despite the allure of certain "false idols," moral truth is not related to money or the things or pleasures money can buy. Rather, what can be stated as true as a matter of opinion must necessarily be traced to, and be consistent with, our human nature.

False Idols Leading away from Truth

Let's take a brief look at some things that get in the way of a family seeing objective moral truth:

Money. Much of modern life is dominated by one of two concerns: the more efficient use of money or its wider distribution. Even a public-policy idea as compassionate sounding as "universal health care coverage" seems to founder on these concerns. Those opposed to such coverage believe it will be inefficient because standard benefits don't fit every family or because it will drive large numbers of small employers out of business. In contrast, many supporters of universal coverage see the mandate to have insurance provided across the board as a way of moving money from the wealthy to the less affluent.

As a law teacher, I can report that virtually every law school in the country is dominated by faculty (and hence students) caught up in one or both of these concerns. Schools of philosophy and political science and business and marketing and accounting are driven by these considerations as well. The object of much university instruction is simply either how to create wealth (and its best-known sibling, power) or distribute it.

Outside the university, money is no small matter either. The expansion of lotteries, off-track betting, the attraction of Las Vegas, Atlantic City, and riverboat gambling, and any one of a large number of other "get rich quick" schemes highlight money's significance. Few families turn away from money, and most have some legitimate need for a greater amount. Moreover, as families, we worry about money all the time: Is there enough to pay the mortgage, to send our children to college, to provide for us when we are ill or disabled? Money appears to be an escape from these worries, and may even be escape from daily routine. The desire for "enough money" to retire early suggests that many Americans want something other than that which they find daily at work on the line in the factory, or behind the check-out counter at K-Mart or even in fancy, professional offices.

The concern with wealth thus does have some importance, but it is fair to say that few of us would want to have our lives summed up or solely identified with it. "Here lies Ebeneezer Scrooge. He amassed big bucks." How ignoble such an epitaph is, especially when compared with the tombstone tributes for those our nation rightly memorialize. Take, for example, Mr. Jefferson's inscription: "the founder of the University of Virginia, the author of the Declaration of Independence and the Virginia Declaration of Religious Freedom." The innate desire to be known by something other than our monetary worth aptly illustrates why money is not a source of absolute moral good or truth. For all of our preoccupation with it, wealth is a means, not an end. While few of us would turn down money, most of us recognize that it creates its own burdens (taxes, problematic investments, overindulgence in food or leisure). In any event, money cannot be the anchor for truth because it is only a surrogate—for obtaining power (this is what politicians seem to do with money) or *other* things and activities (what the rest of us do with money).

What Money Can Buy. It may be thought, then, that power or items and activities that we come to desire out of our culture is the ultimate moral value. Many think so, and lead their lives positioning themselves in places of authority or indulging one pleasure or another or acquiring thing after thing. A moment's reflection, however, should remind us that no one has yet proven to be irreplaceable even in the highest office, vacations come and go (with the weather being too hot or too cold), the bigger house inevitably isn't big enough (or maybe it's too big), and so forth. Positions and things bring, at most, transient satisfaction.

There is another difficulty with trying to look for truth in what money can buy. Specifically, what pleases me displeases you, and who is to say that you're right and I'm wrong. Take an extreme example. The drug addict is pleased by access to crack cocaine, and he implements his desire by robbing others at the point of a gun to obtain money for his habit. Obviously, the addict is temporarily satisfied or pleased, if you will, but no one would seriously characterize him as a moral actor who has located the source of objective truth.

Thankfully, the above example is an extreme or distant one for most Americans, who live their lives pursuing happiness in less flamboyant and felonious ways. But it would be wrong to see the truth failing or moral failing of the addict as related solely to his use of force and not also his mistaken attempt to find truth in what he desires, even if the desire is satisfied without harming others— that is, following the Golden Rule of doing unto others as we would have them do unto us.

Living by the Golden Rule. Many of us grew up on the Golden Rule. To this day, we can hear parents saying, "How would you like it if your brother did that to you?" The point of course was to treat others in the manner we would wish to be treated ourselves. The Golden Rule works well enough as a moral guide because most of us—out of self-interest—want to be treated well, not poorly. But a modern society characterized by increased levels of drug and alcohol use and even suicide reveals the shortcomings of the Golden Rule as a source of objective truth.

Specifically, the Golden Rule only works if it itself is directed at objective moral truth. If applied to the *wrong* objective, the Golden Rule does little to return us to the path of virtuous behavior. For example, our hypothetical drug addict may not be an armed robber but an independently wealthy heir to a private fortune. He can indulge his habit quite easily without undertaking any activity which we would say harms others or which he wouldn't be quite happy having other people "do unto him"—namely, give him large amounts of cash for chemical substances. The Golden Rule is seemingly satisfied, and he is pleased by the drug. No harm. No foul. Only one problem: He feeds cocaine into his system until his health is threatened or ruined. Because modern culture is highly individualistic, we may say that the wealthy addict's plight is unfortunate but of his own choosing. It is none of our business. A so-called "victimless" crime. A few objections might be raised because his self-induced addiction imposes unnecessary costs on the health system (e.g., he is taking up a hospital bed that a "real" sick person deserves), but little else would be said.

This is private, subjective morality run rampant. If pressed to analyze the situation carefully in terms of the "Family Checklist in the Event of Moral Doubt" included earlier in this chapter, it can be safely ventured that hardly any thinking person would conclude that the wealthy addict made a good or wise choice. Drug use doesn't make good use of talents; it merits no honor; it relieves no one else's misfortune; it is likely contrary to the tenets of religion; and unless his mind is totally blown by the drug, even the addict would want to dissuade his closest loved one from following his example. In short, what we desire, even if we observe the Golden Rule to get it, cannot be the measuring rod for goodness or the knowable truth. Some things we desire may be good for us; others bad.

Experience. If money, what it buys, and even the Golden Rule are eliminated as sources of moral truth, a family may be tempted to fall back on muddling through—that is, the pragmatism of day-to-day life. In other words, it may be thought that each person and each family can only come to know that which is good and bad (true or false) *for them* through their actual, particular experience. In the 18th century, John Locke, argued that this is the entire way of learning—"at birth, [each individual] resembles a blank tablet, on which experience marks a series of impressions. These impressions gradually are formed into general ideas. No innate ideas exist . . . ."[5]

The notion that human beings are "blank slates" may sound innocent enough in the abstract, but it is a mischievous one. Why? First, because it is the lazy man's path—a kind of making it up as you go along. If the members of the family fall into good company outside the family and have their "slates" filled accordingly (the odds of which get increasingly longer each day in the culture at large), then truth and personal virtue may be stumbled upon. However, given today's hostile cultural climate, it is just as likely that a family with only a blank slate of personal experiences to guide it will stumble for the worse. Second, and more fundamentally, the blank slate of experience is unacceptable as a source of moral truth because at its very heart, it stands for the proposition that there is no common humanity, and, thus, no common culture. "Taken to its extreme consequences, this individualism leads to a denial of the very idea of human nature."[6]

This is not to say that much of what individuals and families do is uninformed by daily experience. This is one of the ways we learn. But it should be apparent that if *all* we know comes merely from experience, such cannot be the source of objective truth—that is, truth which is immutable and universal—good for all times and places apart from individualized experience. Since experience varies from person to person, it cannot serve as the standard or source for truth itself.

The false idols—money, what money can buy, the Golden Rule, and experience—are not the basis for objective truth in regard to matters of opinion. What is? It has already been disclosed—human nature.

Human Nature—The Touchstone of a Knowable Truth

There was an old saying at the time of the American founding:

---

5   Russell Kirk, *The Roots of the American Order*, 3d ed.(Washington, D.C.: Regnery Gateway, 1991), p. 289. Locke's thinking on this can be found in John Locke, *An Essay concerning Human Understanding*, Bk. I.

6   John Paul II, *The Splendor of Truth* (Veritatis Splendor) (Boston: St. Paul Books & Media, 1993), §32, p. 49.

> Live by the old Ethicks and the classical Rules of Honesty. Put
> no new names or notions upon Authentick Virtues and Vices.
> Think not that Morality is Ambulatory; that Vices in one age
> are not Vices in another; or that Virtues, which are under the
> everlasting Seal of Reason, may be Stamped by Opinion."[7]

Putting aside the quaint spelling in the tradition of the 1700s, the
author of this venerable quotation properly emphasizes the need
for a standard for values that is more timeless than human experience. Indeed, it actually precedes experience. That source is the
essence of our human nature.

Now, introducing human nature as a settled factor of reality
against which matters of opinion can be measured may suggest
that I am once again locating truth in religion—namely, God's
creation of men and women. That would, in my judgment, be a
proper location for any truth claim. Belief in God facilitates understanding. The truth of one's own reality is more readily grasped by
men and women who recognize that they are not self-created,
assembled at random from a buffet line of components with no
ultimate end or design, but intricately designed and part of an
order that originates with God. In itself, the acknowledgment of
Creation goes a long way to explain why each person is deserving
of respect and consideration. If nothing else, the awesome nature
of Creation, which neither Darwin nor any other modern scientist
can fully explain or deny, instills a humility for the power and
intelligence of the Being that lies behind the universe. "Without
[his] Creator[,] the creature simply disappears. . . ."[8]

But, of course, it must be observed that seekers of truth may be
nonbelievers. Thus, it is possible to assume that there is no hard,
scientific proof of how we were created. This, of course, is not just
assumption. Evolution or "Big Bang" theories of creation are every
bit a matter of faith as is the book of Genesis. That said, the
assumption does not block the ascertainment of truth. However we
arrived at our present state of existence, we *do have* a present state
of existence. And the *truth* is, that state of existence or nature can
either be enhanced or destroyed by actions that we take. Thus, it
can be confidently stated that the acquisition of knowledge is better

---

7   Russell Kirk, *supra*, p. 293, referencing Thomas Browne's *Christian
      Morals.*

8   John Paul II, *The Splendor of Truth, supra*, §39, p. 55.

than the consumption of poison. *This is not merely opinion*, and it is definitively proven in relation to our nature as human persons.

Regardless of the *how* of creation, then, before we have any life experience, we had a nature. This nature needs sleep, healthful food, and exercise to physically advance. It requires the pursuit of knowledge to achieve mental accomplishment. We can deliberately choose to ignore these requirements of our nature, but we do so at the cost of diminishing or harming ourselves.

Does this bring us back to the proposition that what we desire is the basis of truth? No. But it does suggest that some things we desire (proper food, rest, knowledge, and so forth) do have a correlation with an objective reality, our natures. This correlation is very important for it specifies the difference between what we *need* and what we merely *want*. What we need is related to our natures as human persons. These natures do not differ from person to person or place to place or time to time. They are universal. In contrast, what we want is a function of our surroundings, for example, wealth, language, and an infinite range of other variables, which do differ in these respects.

Have we located a standard for objective truth in the constancy of human nature? Yes. Before we said that what was factually true did not depend upon our independent opinion of the facts. The Cubs lack of success could be checked in the record books regardless of the delusions of their fans. The proof of *factual* truth rested with the certainty that any statement could be checked against the actual facts to see if it is true. Now we see how the opinion of what is good or bad can be checked as well. While there are no record books, there *is* a designed human nature, and this knowable truth is the "self-evident" principle affirmed in the American Declaration of Independence.

Recognition of a knowable truth, like affirmation of belief in God, also underscores the important distinction between law and morality. It is commonplace in modern, lawsuit-happy America to hear someone say: "They're violating my rights." This expression can be used in many different ways and contexts, but the discussion of a knowable truth and its relationship to human nature should reveal that not all claims of "right" are equal. Some of the "rights" that we have under law are traceable to needs directly related to human nature, and some are traceable merely to wants or preferences that have been enacted into law by a legislature or declared to exist in law by judges at a particular time. Today, we may have claims based upon preferences to various monetary benefits, scenic views over property owned by our neighbors, and even special consideration in employment based on race or gender or disability. Most of these are legislated rights, not truth claims. This distinction is vitally important to the integrity of the law, itself, for it separates those rights that are sufficiently connected to human nature that they should be recognized as a human—or in a proper case constitutional—right, from those that are merely premised upon the tastes of a particular group of lawmakers.

When only want, i.e., taste or preference, lies behind law, it is essential that legislative discretion not be exercised in a manner that contradicts an aspect of the knowable truth. A legislature may desire a highly productive workforce, but to mandate into law that every person work seventy or more hours per week is to impose obligations contrary to our health or natures and, ultimately, antagonistic to the American family. Of course, there may be argument over what our natures truly need. This is to be expected. As earlier mentioned, these disagreements reflect the imperfection or limits of our reason and our ability to perceive reality. Nevertheless, premature or forced resolution of these disputes in law or in claimed "legal rights" leads directly and intractably to the culture war. **In cases of profound disagreement, courts and legislatures should remain silent, allowing particular resolution of these disputes within each family and church.**

The chapters that follow strive to apply or implement this call to cultural virtue. The chapter immediately following focuses on the special case of education. The public education system in many ways epitomizes the manner in which the culture war has been unnecessarily aggravated by displacement of the two mega-virtues. Subsequent chapters detail the vocabulary of the personal cardinal virtues—prudence, courage, temperance, and justice—suggesting practical ways these can be learned and applied in the family. Chapter 9 assesses the structural health of the family itself. A final chapter gives a number of concluding perspectives on the American family. Families must know themselves, what is expected of them and how well those expectations are being met, before the pursuit of personal virtue can be undertaken.

A final word—my own imperfect reason or understanding of God's instruction may lead you to disagree in whole or in part with my applications. If so, let me hear from you. No culture war will result from such correspondence or disagreement since the views expressed are not matters of law or asserted right but one father's effort to recognize the knowable truth and see his family thrive in as much of God's light as has been given him.

Chapter 6

Teaching Virtue—Separation of Church and State Must Not Mean Separation of Family and Education

THE PRE-SCHOOL YEARS PASS very quickly. No sooner does infant crying stop and big wheels are in the driveway. Almost before one can say "Barney," the first day of kindergarten and elementary school is at hand. It leaves a lasting memory picture in the minds of both parent and child. It is indeed a turning point. After this, instructional duties that had been retained exclusively by the parents will be shared with an agent, the teacher.

For far too many children, this first-day experience is being pushed back earlier and earlier into the pre-school years or even infancy. An increasing number of fathers and mothers with demanding jobs or professional careers deposit infants and toddlers in full-time day-care establishments within days or weeks of birth. Reliable evidence suggests that these "latch-key" toddlers are not well-served by the loss of their parental instructors at this early age.[1] These children have more health problems; they are more likely to be aggressive and uncooperative; and tracking them later in school, they perform less well academically.[2]

---

1   Jay Belsky, "Early Human Experience: A Family Perspective," *Developmental Psychology*, 17 (1981), pp 3-23; Urie Bronfenbrenner, *The Ecology of Human Development: Experiments by Nature and Design* (Cambridge, Mass.: Harvard University Press, 1979); Edward Zigler and Winnie Berman, "Discerning the Future of Early Childhood Intervention," *American Psychologist*, 38 (1983), pp. 894–906; Edward Zigler and Matia Finn-Stevenson, *Children: Development and Social Issues* (Lexington, Mass.: D. C. Heath, 1987).

2   See Jay Belsky, "Infant Day Care: A Cause for Concern?" *Zero to Three*, 6 (No. 5 1986), pp. 1-7; Bryce J. Christensen, *Utopia against the Family*

The culture has shifted away from the needs of especially young children to the desires of adult fulfillment. This is not unrelated to the culture war. When parental commitment and instruction of children is unstable and inconsistent, there is a greater likelihood of delinquency and moral breakdown.[3] Conversely, if there is a strong "parent as first teacher," then the child's later commitment to civic responsibility is likely to be strong and positive as well.

Whether fathers and mothers are prepared to re-think their career choices to devote greater efforts toward child-rearing is taken up in Chapter 9. But whether that readjustment occurs or not, parents need to exercise special care in the selection of their teaching-delegate, the school teacher. As one writer put it well, parents must "[b]ecome deeply acquainted with [their] child's teachers . . . . The school is only as good as the parents behind it, and the standards of any school are only as high as the parents demand."[4]

Family Prescription

  * The school chosen for a child must be a genuine
    extension of the family

Every child is unique. Every family is too. Families have distinct histories, occupations, and religious commitments. Yet, from the standpoint of cultural harmony, there must be respect for those things which bind us together. There must be a desire to advance the common welfare, the common good. In earlier chapters, we have discussed the mega-virtues of belief in God and a knowable truth. When the public school system took hold in the 19th century, it was evident that many fine teachers thought the system would nourish exactly these mega-virtues and instill in children what is today called civic virtue. Unfortunately, there is some evidence in the late 19th century that this noble pursuit became partially distorted by bias and fears generated by the large influx of Catholic

(San Francisco: Ignatius Press, 1990), pp. 73–76; Christensen, "Sorokin: Prophet of Family Decay," *The Family in America*, 8 (April 1993); "A Mother's Love: What Children Will Not Receive in Day-Care Centers," *The Family in America*, 8 (December 1993).

3   James Q. Wilson and Glenn C. Loury, eds., "From Children to Citizens," *Families, Schools and Delinquency Prevention*, Vol. 3 (Springer-Verlag, 1987)

4   William Sears, M.D., *Christian Parenting and Child Care*, rev. ed. (Nashville: Thomas Nelson, 1991), p. 411.

and Jewish immigrants. These "foreign" people had to be "Americanized," sometimes in ways that were quite unmindful and disrespectful of ethnic and religious cultures.

While this is not the place to trace the history of the public schools, it is clear that part of the public school philosophy, at least with respect to these newly arrived Americans, was to separate family and education. It was not a complete separation, however, because the early public school philosophy still adhered to the mega-virtues, and those virtues were largely compatible, or at least not inconsistent, at a more general (if Protestantly flavored) level with the particular ethnic and religious ancestries of the families themselves. As one big-city mayor reflects, all worked rather well so long as the mega-virtues supplied a type of "'civil religion' [which] provided the structure for a sound educational system, built on principles the vast majority of Americans would accept."[5]

But then came the 1960s, and with it a Supreme Court jurisprudence that raised the wall of separation between church and state to virtually absolute proportions. Nowhere was this felt more strongly than in the public school system. As understood by the Court, a nation founded on belief in God suddenly could not draw any distinction based on God. As one constitutional law professor observed: "It [did] not seem to bother the Court that this suspension of judgment on the existence of God results in a governmental preference of agnosticism, which is now recognized by the Court as a non-theistic religion."[6]

Today, we are still a nation of believers, though of many religions. In light of this pluralism of belief, there *is* merit in the Court's decisions insofar as they prevent the coercion of religious belief or practice under penalty of law. But that said, whatever is the justifiable extent of church-state separation, that separation must not be allowed by families to create greater distance between their particular religious faith and the education of their children. This is especially true now in the midst of cultural hostility because for a family of believers, a genuine religious commitment can mean the difference between educational success and failure. Enrolling children in a religiously affiliated school helps in two ways: First, the very fact of the affiliation makes the school an extension of the

---

5 Philip F. Lawler, "Breaking the Logjam?" *The Catholic World Report* (July 1994), p. 44.

6 Charles E. Rice, "We Hold No Truths"? *Triumph*, 11 (September 1968), p. 13.

family. They fly under the same flag as it were. Within this shared religious community of family and school, student educational achievement tends to surpass that obtainable in a public or non-religious private school. Second, the substance of religious instruction itself is frequently of considerable assistance to the development of personal virtue and social responsibility. Both points are discussed more fully below.

Family Prescription

> * The school chosen by the family should share the family's religious faith.

It has already been observed how the early separation of parent from child in the pre-school years may impede a child's emotional and educational development. At some point, most parents (except those willing or able to undertake homeschooling), must rely upon full-time teachers for the instruction of their children. Obviously, this too creates time and physical separation from the family. But this separation is far less problematic from the standpoint of educational, emotional, or spiritual development if the children are enrolled in schools that share the religious faith of the family.

The educational success story of religious schools has been documented most prominently with respect to Catholic parochial (or parish) schools, but the results are not faith-specific. A good summary of this research can be found in a recent book published by Harvard University Press.[7] Students in religious schools have significantly lower drop-out rates and higher verbal and mathematical achievement scores. It appears that the secret of this success is not better facilities, resources, or the self-selection of better students. Almost uniformly, Catholic schools operate on a fraction of the money available in public schools. For example, in one state it was recently reported that Catholic schools spend $3,500 or less per student compared with a state average of $10,000 per student in the public school system. As for the argument that religious schools "skim" the best and the brightest, the claim according to researchers "cannot withstand examination." For example, one Michigan study found that "students who attend Detroit area private schools reflect the surrounding geographical areas which

---

7   Anthony S. Byrk, Valerie E. Lee, and Peter B. Holland, *Catholic Schools and the Common Good* (Cambridge, Mass.: Harvard, 1993).

by and large were relatively poor, low-income and in some cases middle-income areas."[8]

So what explains the positive levels of educational achievement and lower drop-out rates in religiously-affiliated schools? It turns out that it is the religious-affiliation itself, and the fact that it is shared by parent and school."[9]

Why Does Religious Affiliation Matter to Educational Achievement?

There is a protracted debate in the public school system over whether inputs (per-pupil expenditures, class size, teacher salaries, age of building and equipment) or outputs (what students actually learn) ought to form the basis of judging educational quality.[10] Why this inputs-outputs question for professional educators is hard to resolve is a bit of a mystery as any parent would supply student achievement as the correct answer in an instant. Apparently, teachers unions and purveyors of educational gadgets tend to muddy the waters. Be that as it may, the research comparing public and religious schools reveals that the best outputs in terms of student achievement are far less related to what is spent on education than the existence of a religious community tying family and school together. This shared religious affiliation results in the close and continuing involvement of parents, and this "social capital" means far more to academic success than the financial capital of either the family (whether they are rich or poor) or the school institution (including teacher salaries or the school's library and facilities). Surprisingly, the "social capital" of the shared religious affiliation even appears to overcome "input" weaknesses in the family structure itself. In this respect, James Coleman found that children in religiously affiliated schools from single-parent households or where both parents work were also less likely than their public school counterparts to drop out of school. In Dr. Coleman's sociological words, "[t]he social capital in the religious community

8   Harry Hutchinson, "Private Schools: Let Competition Heat Up," in "Educational Choice for Michigan," *Mackinac Center Report* (September 1991), p. 57.

9   James S. Coleman, "The Creation and Destruction of Social Capital: Implications for the Law," 3 *Notre Dame J. of L. and Pub. Pol.* 375 (1988).

10   See generally, Frederick Mosteller and Daniel Patrick Moynihan eds., *On Equality of Educational Opportunity* (New York: Vintage, 1972).

surrounding the school appears especially effective for those children lacking strong social capital within the family.[11]

The Vital Role of Parents in Education

The continued involvement of parents in the religious community that surrounds a religious school encourages the child's unique potential in ways that cannot be duplicated in most public school classrooms. It also ensures greater supervision of the child's individual effort, and the accountability of his or her instructors. In essence, the religious affiliation makes the extension of the family into the school years possible. In this way, parents remain the ultimate guarantors against their children becoming lost in the crowd or, if you will, standardized. Despite the confusions of its church-state cases, the Supreme Court long ago formally recognized the preeminent parental role in education. The Court wrote: "[t]he child is not the mere creature of the State; those [parents] who nurture him and direct his destiny have the right, coupled with the high duty, to recognize and prepare him for additional obligations. . . ."[12]

The preeminence of the parental role, of course, must not be abused. When we speak of maintaining a strong connection between family and school, and especially a family's religious tradition and school, it is not a license to instill anti-social beliefs or to keep children locked in "cults" of the David Koresh variety that threaten the public order or the health and well-being of the children themselves. But by the same token, it is overstatement to insist that separate Hebrew and Catholic and Lutheran and Evangelical and Pentecostal and Baptist schools tear at the American fabric. Indeed, quite the opposite is true. Allowing the freedom for these religious groupings to flourish is the very pattern of the American fabric. Attempts to submerge the separate manner in which Americans freely chose to worship God and to educate themselves or their families in conformity with religious belief will only leave the national fabric bleached and ill-fitting.

How Religious Schools Help End the Culture War

This brings us to how the substance of religious instruction itself

---

11   Coleman, *supra*, p. 382.

12   *Pierce v. Society of Sisters* 252 U.S. 239, 535 (1925); see William Bentley Ball, *Mere Creatures of the State?* (Notre Dame, Ind.: Crisis Books, 1994).

can advance cultural harmony. I will admit that at first blush, substantive religious instruction and education appear to travel down different roads. The purpose or central objective in the study and practice of religion is salvation; reunification and eternal life with God, Who is described in much religious teaching as the very definition of love and goodness. In this, religion is a counter-cultural force; that is, one which takes exception to those worldly matters and concerns which deflect us from our intended end. Stephen Carter properly calls religion an "independent source of power" or a necessary "nose-thumber" even in a democracy.[13] By contrast, education is an embrace of culture. It is all about the world—from the geography of countries to the full range of basic skills in reading, mathematics, language, the physical properties of matter and so on. Again, it is for the development of these latter competencies that parents are most needful of specialists—namely, teachers.

However, a complete education must involve more than basic competencies or the acquisition of skills; it must also aid in the formation of moral character. The success or failure of America as a government and as a democratically organized culture depend upon the moral development of its people, and especially its school children. That is why the Northwest Ordinance of 1787, the governing document shaping the early territorial expansion of the United States, deliberately linked "religion, morality, and knowledge [as] being necessary to good government and the happiness of mankind." From the view of America's founding generation, religion and education were inseparable. Is there reason to conclude that this is no longer true in the 1990s?

The evidence is to the contrary. On the competency or basic-skills side of the education equation, the demonstrated success of religiously affiliated schools has already been discussed. It is equally well documented that many American public schools are failing in matters of skills and competency. Report after report confirms our nation's public "educational foundations" to be presently "eroded by a rising tide of mediocrity that threatens our very future as a Nation and a people."[14] In recent international competitions, American students on nineteen academic tests never fin-

---

13 Stephen L. Carter, *The Culture of Disbelief* (New York: Basic Books, 1993), p. 35.

14 *A Nation at Risk*, The National Commission on Excellence in Education (Washington, D.C.: Government Printing Office, 1983), p. 5.

ished first or second and, "when compared with other industrial-
ized nations, were last seven times."[15] On most standardized tests,
the average achievement of high school students is less than the
comparable student thirty years ago. When the National Geo-
graphic Society tested eighteen-to-twenty-four year olds, the *New
York Times* reported that America finished dead last among the ten
nations tested, with even 14 percent of the Americans unable to
find the United States on a world map.[16]

The moral formation side of the education equation in many
public schools is little better. A few years ago, government statistics
revealed that *each* month close to 300,000 students and over 5,000
teachers were attacked in public schools.[17] It is frightfully commonplace for school administrators to discover students carrying weap-
ons. As former Chief Justice Warren Burger laments, "[d]ays in
school with dedicated teachers and eager students struggling to
master their lessons have given way, all too often, to disorder and
a gripping fear by teachers and students."[18] Obviously, this increased level of violence and disruption in public school only
aggravates the decline in academic achievement and makes more
remote any chance for its reversal.[19] Among other things, school
violence rationally convinces some to avoid coming to school
entirely, an invitation all too willingly accepted by marginal students.[20]

Religiously affiliated schools accept far less bad behavior before
bringing in parents or exacting academic and corporal penalties.
Because these schools are not arms of the government, it is still
possible for discipline to be imposed without triggering claims that
some constitutional right has been violated, such as legal rights to
formal notice and hearing, counsel, or a dispassionate, disinter-

---

15   The Mackinac Center Report, *supra*, p. 5, citing the National Com-
     mission on Excellence in Education.

16   The Mackinac Center Report, *supra*, p. 6, citing the *New York Times* of
     November 9, 1989.

17   *National School Safety Center News Journal* (Winter 1987), cited in
     Gregory L. Evans, "School Crime and Violence: Achieving Deter-
     rence through Tort Law," 3 *Notre Dame J. of L. and Pub. Pol.* 501, 502
     (1988).

18   Warren Burger, "School Safety Goes to Court, *School Safety* (Winter
     1986), pp. 4–5.

19   National Institute of Justice, *Violence in Schools* (December 1986), p.
     2.

20   Evans, *supra*, p. 503.

ested decision-maker. I must confess that I smiled as I wrote this last sentence because I can recall getting "paddled" on the spot (not a whole lot of notice) by a Christian Brother in high school who indicated in the course of publicly administering this penalty that he was indeed greatly interested in my welfare. My offense, by the way, was studying for a French language examination during choral practice. Ouch, or at least, *Ou est la biblioteque!*

But even more important than the flexibility and discretion that private religious schools retain in matters of discipline is the moral instruction that makes much discipline unnecessary. This moral teaching is very often both highly compatible with the sustenance of a common American culture and respectful of a family's religious tradition. Take, for example, the following passages from a civics book published in 1951 and intended for use in the third or fourth grade in Catholic schools:[21]

* *on the basis for American government*: the book compares the work of Cardinal Bellarmine, who wrote centuries before Jefferson, to illustrate how American democracy is consistent with religious thinking. Bellarmine: "[s]ecular or civil power is instituted by men; it is in the people, unless they bestow it on the prince . . . ." Jefferson: "governments are instituted among men, deriving just powers from the consent of the governed."[22]

* *on the importance of ethical business practice*: "In the field of business there are many obstacles to the practice of virtue. . . . [H]onesty, fairness, justice, and charity must be the motivating spirit, rather than the desire for financial gain. It is the duty of the Church to promote the practice of these virtues. From this point of view, '*Business* is definitely the business of the Church.'"[23]

* *on the environment*: the book traces natural resources to God and decries wasteful over-consumption and environmental degradation. After outlining the efforts of the federal government, the volume discusses the needs of the environment in terms that would make tangible sense to an eight year old within a family context;

---

21   Archdiocese of Chicago, *Christian Civics* (Chicago: Mentzer, Bush and Co. 1951).

22   *Id.*, p. 67.

23   *Id.*, p. 225.

for example, the book provides its own checklist "to practice justice by conserving resources," including "leaving places in good condition when [children] visit parks," being "reasonable and careful in the use of public equipment," and keeping conservation in mind while fishing, hunting or gardening. The section concludes: "[a] respect for all the forms of our God-given resources—all the beauties of life and nature—will be the strongest foundation for our spirit of conservation."[24]

* *on family life and personal responsibility*: "It isn't the kind of work you do around the house that matters so much. It is the fact that you take responsibility of a fair share of it. . . . In a good home citizens learn to live wisely and democratically. Each family member tries to respect the rights of others. . . . Fair sharing of family possessions makes for happiness of the individuals and is excellent training for the wider responsibilities of citizenship. . . . To keep the members of your family interested in home affairs is a sure way of preserving the unity of the family. In choosing forms of recreation you should try to discover interests which both you and your parents can share."[25] (Beavis and Butthead, step aside!)

Overall, this slender volume aimed at relatively young children stresses how civic duty and spiritual responsibility are necessarily integrated. Such integration of the moral and intellectual may not be politically correct from the standpoint of an educational bureaucrat imposing a uniform, faceless and often lifeless view from afar, but it is correct and effective as a personal extension of the family and the family's religious belief into every aspect of a child's upbringing and activity. I'll let the book speak for itself:

> "The Church takes an active part in promoting the general welfare. Since the supernatural life, which the Church nourishes, is the complete life for man, supernatural standards and objectives must be sought in everything man does. Thus it becomes the duty of the Church to point out the supernatural standards and rules affecting industry, art, politics, business, law, medicine, and whatever else is a part of modern living. All things must be directed to God if they are 'to promote the general welfare.'"[26]

---

24   *Id.*, p. 200.

25   *Id.*, p. 26.

26   *Id.*, p. 224.

The teaching of religious schools as exemplified by the words of this common civics book is promotive of American culture, practically instructive in matters of basic knowledge and personal responsibility, and yet entirely consistent with the religious worldview of the family. The child is not uncomfortably forced to live two lives—one at home and the other at school. Most importantly, the child is not pressured into abandoning one or the other source of teaching. Parental instruction is reaffirmed and elaborated by the religious school. The health of our culture depends on far more than the minimalist objective of keeping guns out of the classroom or the certification of vague "opportunity to learn standards" by the U.S. Department of Education under recently enacted "Goals 2000 Educate America Act."[27] The famed educator Rudolf Steiner credited with identifying the importance of early childhood education stated it in these eloquent terms:

> "If one observes children who, by right upbringing, have developed a natural reverence for the grownups in their surroundings, and if one follows them through their various stages of life, one can discover that their feelings of reverence and devotion in childhood are gradually being transformed during the years leading to old age. As adults such persons may have a healing effect upon their fellow-men so that by a single glance they can spread inner peace to others. Their presence can be a blessing because as children they have learned to venerate and to pray in the right way. No hands can bless in old age, unless in childhood they have been folded in prayer."[28]

So Why, then, Is the Family's Religion Separated from Education?

The simple answer, suggested earlier, is the difficulty the Supreme Court has had reconciling the constitutional provision barring the establishment of religion with religion's obvious connection to the type of moral instruction that must occur in school if the school is to faithfully be the extension or teaching agent of the parent. This is not the place to exhaustively present the legal argumentation. That has been done elsewhere.[29] It is enough to say

---

27   Bruno V. Manno, "Outcome-Based Education—Miracle Cure or Plague?" *Hudson Briefing Paper* (June 1994), p. 10.

28   Rudolf Steiner, *The Renewal of Education* (Forest Row, U.K.: Steiner Schools Fellowship Publications, 1981), p. 65.

that the operative understanding of the Court's legal direction as implemented by public school administrators is that no mention of religion may be made by teachers other than perhaps in passing or comparative reference in a history course. Of late, the Court has seemingly approved voluntary, spontaneous student prayer,[30] but this is so contested by the ACLU that many school administrators frown on this as well. In terms of the original understanding of the Constitution, this is error insofar as the "no establishment" prohibition refers to the coercion of religious belief and practice under law, not to the mere reference to religion. But error or not, it practically has meant that teachers have been forbidden to have the Bible on their desks, to include religious materials or books in classroom libraries, or even to allow a student to voluntarily read a passage from the Book of Genesis as that student's favorite reading selection—at least without parental intervention and advice of counsel.

It must be admitted, however, that the larger problem for purposes of this chapter is less traceable to the mistakes of constitutional interpretation than the basic incompatibility of religious belief and the idea of public or government schools. When the government speaks officially, people listen—because they have to. But what can a government that is properly neutral among religious denominations have to say about religion or virtue to be derived from specific religious teaching? Very little beyond token references to God. Starved for virtue and the practical application of religious teaching to their day-to-day lives, many families (the vast majority of Americans if polling data is accurate)[31] support the idea of public school prayer. But the content of such prayer will surely never approximate the specific instruction to be found in a religious school. For example, it would likely pale in comparison to the third grade Christian civics instruction quoted earlier. Even were the Court to revise its thinking more in conformity with the original understanding of the founders, the public school context would still pose a seemingly insoluble dilemma because underneath whatever a government school chooses as its prayer is coercion, not the informed, voluntary choice of families.

---

29 See Douglas W. Kmiec, *The Attorney General's Lawyer* (New York: Praeger, 1992).

30 *Lee v. Weisman*, 112 S. Ct. 2649 (1992); *Jones v. Clear Creek*, 983 F. 2d 234 (5th Cir 1992), *cert. denied*, 113 S. Ct. 2950 (1993).

31 *Wall Street Journal* (July 19, 1994), p. A1.

Why Prayer or Generic Value Instruction in Public School Is Not the Answer

True, no public school student is coerced by law to believe anything—and as some wag might say, the test scores show it! Nonetheless, there is the coercion under law in having to be in school. This coercion is aggravated when public resources for education are taxed away from the family and directed to only one educational provider. But even if this more remote or general form of coercion is said to be inconsequential, and thus more meaningful use of religion could be made in a public school without running afoul of the Constitution or its judicial interpretation, the very real practical problem of what denominational source to use in a public institution in the teaching morals would remain.

There is no good answer to this, short of allowing parents to choose freely the school that their children will attend. It is too late in the day to pretend that the public schools can return to some pre-1960s form of homogenized, Protestant moral instruction that may have then infused the school system. Nor would such a return be desirable, as multi-denominational religious instruction is like trying to mix chili and ice cream—it produces distasteful intellectual and spiritual hash. A few members of Congress have vainly sought to return down this path by suggesting laws that would mandate the teaching of generic values without religion. Besides being the equivalent of teaching flying without a plane, these proposals hit a snag the moment someone asks what values are to be taught or how they are to be defined, and why? Because of this, seven times during recent years, Congress has been unable to agree on offering meager demonstration grants to promote honesty, responsibility, and even something insipidly labeled "caring." A few local communities have had better luck in getting past the definitional stage because the values of their local community were still sufficiently tangible and shared within these smaller geographical settings to be identified. However, for Congress to attempt this nationally raises all of the problems mentioned earlier with using law as a substitute for morality, including exacerbated cultural tension and ultimately vapid standards. As Congressman Richard Armey said in opposing one such national effort:

> I for one, would not tolerate anybody having the presumption to dare to think they should define who my children are, what their values are, what their ethics are and who in the hell they will be in this world. The fact is these people don't know my

children and the fact is they don't love my children. And the
fact is they don't care about my children and the further fact
is they accept no responsibility for the outcome . . . and they
ought, by God, leave my kids alone.[32]

Congressman Armey's words have great intensity, and in my
judgment, underscore the reasons why parents must directly and
freely choose their children's schools: teachers come and go while
parents love children always; parents must be free to manifest that
love through one of the most important gifts they can supply—
namely, their specific religious tradition.

It cannot be argued that the present state of public schools allows
this. The very idea of a public school in the modern legal and
cultural context of America is one separated from religion. In this,
the public school can only half-educate. At best (and as noted
earlier there is considerable doubt that many public institutions are
even up to this), public schools can pursue what classical scholars
call the intellectual virtues, namely, competencies in art and science
and mathematics and so forth. This instruction may produce a
good car mechanic or a good accountant or good lawyer; it is not
at all aimed at yielding a good man or woman. Such goodness must
be derived from serious study of the theological virtues of faith,
hope, and charity and the general moral virtues of prudence,
justice, temperance, and fortitude. This simply cannot be done
without sending a child to a school that can introduce these theological and moral virtues in ways that are integrated with the
acquisition of basic skills and compatible with the family's religious preference.

Hey, Parents Can Send their Children to Religious Schools Now!

It may be argued in response that all parents are presently free
to send their children to a religious school; they merely must pay
for it. The facetious nature of this asserted "freedom" was aptly
rebutted by John Lyon in the *Family in America*, one of the Rockford
Institute's excellent publications of assistance to families. Lyon
writes:

32 Rochelle Sharpe, "Efforts to Promote Teaching of Values in Schools
    Are Sparking Heated Debate Among Lawmakers," *Wall Street Jour-
    nal* (March 10, 1994), p. A20.

Just how "free" would we be to exercise our right to provide nourishing food for our children if the government taxed us to support a state chain of comprehensive supermarkets and required that there be one in every "food district" of the state? We might set up peoples' food co-ops until we were blue, but we could not really compete with the government's subsidized chain. The situation might be minimally tolerable if state stores offered quality goods. But if, in our suppositious case, the government decided to purvey largely junk food in its subsidized supermarkets, the situation would be intolerable.[33]

And while we are on the subject of who is free to do what, let me suggest that the notion that has taken hold that it is constitutionally permissible to tax all citizens to create a common fund for education, but to then exclude some citizens on the basis of religious belief is a gross disregard for the free exercise of religion guaranteed by the First Amendment. This unjust and unequal treatment is no more sustainable than if the government set aside tax monies for cancer research, and then pronounced that Lutheran or Baptist physicians, or more broadly any person of faith, need not apply.

Again, it may be claimed that religionists are not excluded from public funds, the government is merely declining to subsidize the constitutional freedom to go to a religious school. There is some facial plausibility to this argument. It falls away, however, as Lyon points out above, when it is recognized that there are different ways to deny freedom, including the very practical one of making families pay twice to act on their religious convictions (once to the government in taxes and once to the private school).

Others may try to finesse the troublesome exclusion of believers from their own money in the public education fund by denying the premise—that is, that attendance at a public school burdens religious belief or practice. This may be true for some families; they could have their children attend the public school without formally transgressing church instruction. For others, however, this is not the case, as readings or other class exercises directly contravene church teaching.[34]

---

33   John Lyon, "Reclaiming the Schools: Reconciling Home and Education," *The Family in America*, 8, No. 6 (June 1994), p. 6.

34   *Mozert v. Hawkins*, 827 F. 2d 1058, 1060–62 (6th Cir. 1987), *cert. den.*,

As one Christian medical doctor explained, "A child left to himself [in a public school] will not choose the path to Christ without some direction from persons of significance around him."[35] In any event, Supreme Court Justices ought not sit in judgment of what any person's religious belief requires, unless public order is directly threatened. The Justices have said as much themselves.[36] For example, the Supreme Court has held that a person cannot be forced to choose between following the dictates of her religion and a government benefit, such as unemployment compensation.[37] Remembering too that the Court has also confirmed the right of parents, not the state, to direct their children's education, it is insupportable to make parents choose between their religion and the only available public support for education in the form of the public school.

In Funding Education, Let Parents Be Parents

The solution for reuniting education and family in the pursuit of virtue is obvious: tax monies for education must once again be brought under direct family control. Of course, so long as its requirements are reasonable ones not aimed at impeding religious belief or practice, the state can mandate that parents have their children educated in certain secular subject areas and through an appropriate age. But the state need not collect and control a family's resources to accomplish these regulatory interests. The easiest way to respect the parents preeminent role in education would be to provide a tax credit to parents for reasonable amounts expended on tuition at the school of their choice. Vouchers are another possibility, but frankly, there is little administrative reason to have the government collect family money only to return it.

But won't this violate the Supreme Court's current "no reference" or exclusion of religion view of the establishment clause? No. The Court itself has acknowledged that generally available public funding may reach religious schools if it is directed there by the choices of individual parents.[38] When individual parents are mak-

---

484 U.S. 1066 (1988).

35   Sears, *supra*, p. 410.

36   *Employment Division v. Smith*, 494 U.S. 872 (1990).

37   *Sherbert v. Verner*, 394 U.S. 398, 403–4 (1963).

38   *Mueller v. Allen*, 463 U.S. 388 (1983); *Witters v. Washington*, 493 U.S. 850 (1989); *Zobrest v. Catalina Foothills School District*, 113 S. Ct. 2462

ing the decisions about how to spend their own funds, it cannot be seriously argued that it is the state that is endorsing or establishing religion.

Once education funding is no longer confiscated and withheld from parents, there will be greater willingness and capability to draw upon religious instruction as part of moral formation. Other educational options would be more doable as well. For example, with the relief given to the family budget by equitable access to the public education fund, the necessity for two family incomes decreases, and homeschooling may become a possibility. Homeschooling has been recognized as an increasingly effective and popular alternative for re-invigorating the family and its teaching of the habits of virtue. An estimated half million children are currently being homeschooled.[39] Students learning at home frequently meet or exceed the educational accomplishments of those in public instruction. For example, "[i]n Oregon, 67% of home schoolers who took national achievement tests during the current school year scored at or above the national public school average."[40]

Not every family will be able or want to home school. But for every child, a family remains the best teacher. When families find meaning in religious faith, education and educational agents outside the home must draw upon that faith too or a child becomes alienated from his or her best instructors and most influential sources. Separation of church and state properly does keep government out of the tenets of faith and, by the same token, particular religious dogma out of government policy. Today, however, separation of church and state is being improperly used to separate family from education. America's religious freedom does not depend upon either diminishing the primary role of parents as the moral educators of their children or inhibiting family religious commitment. In truth, the restoration of America's cultural virtue depends on just the opposite.

(1993).

39   Steve Stecklow, "Fed Up with Schools, More Parents Turn to Teaching at Home," *Wall Street Journal* (May 10, 1994), p. A1.

40   *Id.*

Chapter 7
Families Need Character—
The Teaching of Personal
Virtue

AS ONE NEWS MAGAZINE put it, there is a "craving for virtue . . . ."[1]
That craving has manifested itself in political rhetoric and popular
writing by sociologists, philosophers and even a potential presidential candidate, William Bennett, whose edited *Book of Virtues*,
consisting of classic stories of responsibility, courage, and the like
has sold over a million copies in hardcover. Deservedly so, it is a
superb collection of moral stories and poems from the Bible to
Jefferson to Martin Luther King, Jr., to Robert Frost. Yet, before
politics gets too far out ahead of substance, it is worthwhile exploring exactly what it means for families to instruct in the ways of
virtue or good character.

How Is Virtue Acquired?

There is an age-old dispute between two great philosophers,
Plato and Aristotle, over the issue of the teaching of virtue. At
times, Plato seems to favor the acquisition of virtue through knowledge alone, while Aristotle sounds a bit like Knute Rockne—practice, boys, practice. In Aristotle's terms, "We become just by doing
just acts, temperate by doing temperate acts, brave by doing brave
acts."

In his recounting of the famous dialogues, Plato has the question
put to Socrates directly: "Can you tell me, Socrates, whether virtue
is acquired by teaching or by practice; or if neither by teaching nor
practice, then whether it comes to man by nature, or in some other

---

1   Howard Fineman, "The Virtuecrats," *Newsweek* (June 13, 1994), p. 31.

way?" Socrates answer is something like "all of the above and more." In particular, he answers that virtue cannot be a simple matter of teaching because it is never learned completely. Nor is it only a matter of practice, as Socrates notes that there are too many examples of virtuous fathers who have produced the opposite in their sons. Instead, Plato tells us that Socrates concludes that knowledge and practice are both essential, as is the fact that "virtue comes to the virtuous by the gift of God."

Knowledge, practice, and faith are necessary. Some may dispute including faith. For example, Bill Bennett posits that "you can be a virtuous person without faith in God."[2] Perhaps, but it is surely far more difficult, as Bennett would likely admit. To separate knowledge and practice from faith is to create unhelpful distance between moral formation and what many find to be the most compelling reason for a life well lived—reunification with God. So too excluding faith diminishes the role of the church as a primary instructor in matters of morals. St. Augustine puts it in these strong terms:

> rather [there will be] vices than virtues so long as there is no reference to God in the matter. For although some suppose that virtues have a reference only to themselves, and are desired only on their own account. . . , the fact is that [virtues acquired solely for our benefit] are inflated with pride, and are therefore to be reckoned vices.[3]

Not all have faith, and faith systems differ. Yet, since before Christ, the acquisition of virtue has been a matter of learning, practice, *and* faith. If the culture war is to be ended, each of these avenues will be vitally important. It would be foolhardy, even imprudent to use the moral word, for a family to ignore any source of guidance.

In this chapter and the next, virtue is given concrete definition. Because the audience is families, the emphasis is on the practical and the personal, not the philosophical. Specific checklists or prescriptions are given, but not as an invariable code or because they are the only path to virtue. It will be enough if they are helpful to families in a time of cultural strife.

---

2   *Id.* at 33.

3   Mortimer Adler, *Syntopicon*, 2 (Chicago: Encyclopedia Britannica, Inc., 1991), p. 780, referencing Augustine, *The City of God*, Bk. XIX, ch. 25.

What then Is Personal Virtue?

It is essentially a quality of character, of habit, by which individuals recognize and do that which is right or good. Now the word "habit" is a slippery concept, but it primarily refers to controlling the *mind* by which we think, the *will* or body by which we act, and the *emotions* by which we have certain inclinations or desires, such as those toward food or drink or sexual relations. Habits are useful because they facilitate life's activities. Each time a new situation arises, a new response does not have to be learned but merely drawn out of past moral training. Thus, when we say that a person is naturally trustworthy, we really mean, not that he was born that way, but that he has trained the actions of his mind, body or emotions in that fashion. Like anything that is partially dependent upon practice and self-control, a habit or virtue learned is subject to being un-learned or forgotten, by non-use. Thus, lying also can become habit-forming, as in the expression, "He is a habitual liar."

Virtue—The Key to a Good Life—Now

When examining in an earlier chapter the second mega-virtue— a knowable truth, we saw that men and women have natures. These human natures have defined characteristics, just like a car has a design that facilitates movement by means of wheels, an internal combustion engine, steering and braking mechanisms, and a protective covering. We know that if we deliberately cause or negligently allow any of the parts of our car to malfunction that the car will not perform as it is intended. In short, the car will not be able to fulfill its potential or, if you will, its end. Our human nature too has component parts, a body and soul. The body consists of our physical components—arms, legs, eyes; damage any one of them, and we quickly find out that "living" each day becomes more difficult. When we hobble about on crutches with a broken leg, we have rendered it difficult to be fully human, to fulfill our end, at least in the physical sense of walking.

We work to keep our bodies physically healthy and fit. The acquisition of moral health—the fitness of the soul, if you will—requires similar effort. Like losing weight, it doesn't just happen. The objective of the virtues discussed in this chapter is to advance the moral side of the human person, to make sure that individual human nature is operating at maximum capability. Every day, now.

Virtue and the Next Life

The fitness of the soul? A soul means different things to nonbelievers than it does to believers, but the pursuit of virtue is relevant to both. To a nonbeliever who does not share the believer's recognition of eternity or an afterlife, the meaning of soul is equivalent to life force. Just as a living plant or animal has its requisite life force, so too the soul of a living person is thought of by a nonbeliever as the summation of the essence of a particular person. Thus, when the unique person known as Bob Taylor of 321 Maple in Springdale, Missouri, dies, his physical functions cease. This cessation is tangible and observable, even as mechanical respirators and the like might allow their operations to continue. But there are no human mechanisms for keeping Bob's life force or soul alive. We can keep Bob's body warm and functioning, but once Bob's life force, or higher brain functions, cease, after a very short time, Bob as we knew him is irretrievable. The nonbeliever's use of the word "soul" in this generic, life-force way is neither theological nor religious, but it is related to the acquisition of virtue. An individual's personal qualities are advanced by the acquisition and practice of moral or natural virtues, just as bodily functions are advanced by physical exercise. Employing wise or prudent judgment or remaining temperate in drink, to give two obvious examples, will enhance the functioning of the brain or life force as well as the body.

But the soul has a more expansive meaning for a believer, since faith in God treats the soul as immortal. Insofar as the soul will never die, its end or purpose exceeds all human action, even virtuous ones. Virtuous choices, good deeds here on earth, are helpful to the attainment of eternal life with God, but because the end of eternal life is beyond our natures, literally *super*-natural, something more is required. St. Thomas Aquinas writes: "Now, eternal life is an end which exceeds the proportion of human nature, . . . and therefore man through his natural powers cannot produce meritorious works proportionate to eternal life."[4]

Faith traditions differ on what "something more" is needed. Many rely heavily upon the help of the Holy Spirit; others underscore grace through worship and the receipt of sacraments within the church; still others give great weight to good works. Christian faiths, in general, stress the need to be "born again," referencing

---

4   St. Thomas Aquinas, *Summa Theologica*, I-II, q. 109, a. 5.

the words in John's Gospel where Christ declares: "Believe me when I tell you this: a man cannot see the kingdom of God without being born anew."[5] In the quest to be "born anew," much Christian teaching revolves around the theological virtues of faith, hope, and charity—virtues which are described as putting man in touch directly with God through belief, trust, and love.

These theological virtues are hardly unrelated to bringing the culture war to an appropriate cease-fire. The stronger the instruction in these virtues by church and family, the more likely it is that disputants in the culture war will understand how its wrongful continuation leads away from, not toward, the end of eternal life. In particular, religious instruction which gives emphasis to the possession of Divine Life as part of the sharing of the Body of Christ necessarily submerges cultural division.

Nevertheless, theology and the theological virtues are necessarily beyond the scope of this book aimed as it is at readers of many faiths, and perhaps none at all. The focus here is the very practical: to examine, sometimes in checklist fashion, those human or natural virtues that every parent: should be familiar with; demonstrate in their own lives; and affirmatively teach to their children. Yes, as William Bennett and other political figures say, families need "character"; they need to pursue "traditional values"; but to do that they first need to reacquaint themselves with the substance of virtue itself. For centuries, this substance has been the cardinal virtues.

The Cardinal Virtues

The cardinal virtues—prudence, fortitude (courage), temperance, and justice take their name from the Latin *cardo* for "hinge." On these great virtues, all morality depends. They are the hinge on the door to human perfection. How many American families can even define these terms today, let alone give them practical application to the family? In this chapter, that effort will be made with respect to prudence, fortitude and temperance. The following chapter separately takes up the somewhat more complex virtue of justice.

Prudence
The Prudent man looketh well to his going.
—Proverbs 14:13

5   John 3:3.

As virtues in general are said to direct us to the right or proper end, prudence in particular is aimed at ensuring that we have the right means to that end. In the language of the Book of Proverbs, that we may look well where we are going. A prudent person is one who is willing to take counsel, judge a situation carefully and soundly, and then to direct action in accordance with that judgment.

Seek Advice

None of us know all that we need to know about any subject. Young children exhibit this best by asking seemingly endless questions. As temporarily bothersome as such questions may be, wise parents encourage children to keep asking. It is important for children to seek advice, especially as they get older and enter adolescence. Young children discouraged from asking questions will likely refrain from seeking advice later as teenagers in fear of looking stupid. Of course, the result of the fear of looking stupid is to remain so. When children are faced with difficult cultural issues, such as abortion or peer pressure to have sexual relations outside marriage, parents earnestly want them to come to them for counsel. This is only likely to happen, however, if parents themselves have been open to their children throughout life and have demonstrated their own reliance upon the advice of others. If we are acting prudently, there are many occasions to rely upon the advice and counsel of others. For example, asking the priest or minister for advice with a marriage problem, pursuing the local banker for financial advice in making investments, or even researching consumer information on cars or appliances before making a major purchase.

Believers underscore the importance of seeking advice or deliberating by pointing to the example of Christ, himself. On one level, Jesus is portrayed in the Gospels—in the temple with the money-changers, for example—as commanding, independent, decisive. Yet, at the same time, Jesus shows throughout that He was entirely dependent upon the Father. For example, Jesus says: "The Son can do nothing of himself, but only what he sees the Father doing."[6] In this, it may be said that in our relationship to God, we are called upon to be both well-directed and childlike. Matthew writes: "Unless you turn and become like little children, you will not enter the kingdom of heaven."[7]

---

6   John 5:19.

Judge Wisely

After obtaining advice, it must be impartially assessed. Just as we would not want to be judged in a court of law by a friend of the opposing party, so too in our own lives and the instruction we give our children, we must be as free of prejudice as possible. In personal decisions, prejudice is most likely found in emotion or impulsiveness. The red sports car looks fast or manly or cool; unfortunately, it has terrible gas mileage, a poor service record, and it seats two when you have a family of seven.

Act Accordingly

There is no point seeking advice, sorting and weighing the options, and then disregarding it all. In modern life, disregard often comes in the form of delay—knowing what prudently has to be done (the furnace needs cleaning before winter, for example, but putting it off until it makes that more costly and too-late grinding noise).

Family Check List—Prudence

1. *Be responsive to a child's questions;* the lack of time to give answer today may result in an unwillingness to seek advice tomorrow.

2. *Demonstrate your own reliance upon the advice of others*—spouse, clergy, financial adviser, lawyer. This is especially important for children to see exhibited between spouses. Don't just say, "go ask your mother"; a better response is to say, "I'll talk with your mother about it," and then actually do so.

3. *Think out loud.* When family decisions have to be made, like the purchase of a new car or a household move or which college to attend or even which fast-food restaurant to eat at, weigh the pros and cons together.

4. *Act on good advice received.* Here the essential message is to avoid procrastination when something has to be done for the good of the family. For example, if a child is struggling in mathematics or reading, address the problem before it becomes a larger problem of academic frustration or alienation. Illustrate how saving is the result of financial advice or how a particular car repair is the consequence of consulting the mechanic before the long vacation.

5. *Encourage memory skills.* Often, the most available source of advice is our own experience. Experience teaches, if we only re-

---

7   Matthew 18:3.

member it in advance. Children should be asked each day what they learned at school. A common, but unacceptable, response is: "nothing new." Probing deeper, one often finds at least some new fact or event. Out of what is remembered, a discussion or practical application can result. All knowledge doesn't originate in school alone, of course. Remember the last time you left the window open in a storm? Or the dog was left unattended?

6. *Anticipate needs.* Every fall, new student materials must be purchased. Why not ask children to do the first draft of that list? If summer camp is around the corner, let the children pack, but prudence suggests that you take a look yourself before they exit— too many Butterfinger bars aren't good for anyone. As college nears, have your son or daughter make a list of the features most attractive in any prospective institution to them and explain why. If college isn't planned, what kind of job preparation is going on in high school or vocational school?

7. *Avoid haste.* Things often look different in the morning light. This is true about a job choice, a new home, or the selection of a consumer good. When you really *must* have something or do something, wait and think about it just a little longer than usual. You'll feel the internal struggle; contain your desire with a review of the options until some of the initial compulsion has passed.

8. *Avoid excess.* Aristotle gives us this one, and we know its truth every time we stay up too late, eat or drink too much, or show up unprepared or late for school or the day's work.

9. *Avoid thoughtlessness.* Part of prudence is judging the needs of others around you. In families, the television (if it must be on!) should be moderated in volume to allow others sleep or study or conversation. So too another form of thoughtlessness is to be indiscrete with the confidences of friends or family.

10. *Prudence is not craftiness.* Underlying prudence as a virtue is the understanding that, as a means, it is aimed at a proper end. The last thing a family should do is teach children forms of "planned cheating," such as deliberately underpaying taxes or business obligations or doing poor or sloppy work.

Fortitude

And every one said to his brother,
Be of good courage

—Isaiah 41:6

The virtue of fortitude, or courage, strives for the intermediate course between the extremes of cowardliness and undue boldness. This middle course bids us to seek the good confidently but not foolishly. Defined in the classics as giving the mind and soul sufficient firmness to withstand setback and even danger, fortitude can give family members the strength to come to terms with the culture war. It allows those who genuinely yearn for virtue to continue bravely in the face of scorn, criticism, or even misleading flattery or praise.

Families seeking virtue may be subject to ridicule. Unfortunately at this time, some of this divisive criticism comes even from on high: the president, various members of Congress and some national journalists have lashed out with increasing frequency at the so-called "religious right," a group that apparently does not profess a common faith but does share a common belief that faith is important to life. Attacks by high-ranking or public figures can intimidate. It is courage, the virtue of fortitude, that sustains. So too when we encounter great praise or flattery, a well-developed sense of fortitude keeps these words from "going to our head." In this sense, fortitude is a virtue that allows us to stay on course toward proper ends, distracted neither by fear nor vanity.

Within family life, courage can be practiced by striving for goals without expecting the impossible. Each family member ought to identify goals that can be accomplished in the near and long term and make them known to each other. For a family strong in faith, the overriding goal should be to discover and do God's will. This can take the form of regular attendance as a family at worship, personal and family prayer, the study of Scripture and the specifics of one's faith. Above all, it means a family dedicated to serving God openly, even when that may subject the family to ridicule as less arduous and more tempting courses of action present themselves.

Beyond the importance of keeping God behind each of our goals, how—practically—can this identification of personal objectives be done? Start out by listing the loftiest aspiration for yourself and each family member. Have the others in the family do the same. Then, talk at length about them. These aspirations should be entirely candid. For example, I have made it well-known to the family my desire to write a book bolstering the confidence and strength of the family in the midst of cultural attack. That is a goal, and if you are reading these words, it turned out to be relatively short term. Explaining why this goal was important to me allowed others in the family to walk with me more closely in life and bolster my spirits—to *encourage*—when the task seemed impossible. We need to know ourselves and let other family members know us without the masks we wear before others outside the family.

Not everything will be an intellectual goal. My teenage son has taken to the game of golf. It is his aspiration to be as good as his grandfather, who plays regularly in his retirement. As hard as it is for the rest of the family to identify with my son's interest, we good-naturedly listen and inquire about his backswing and the like. The good in this, as we tell him, is the physical exercise he receives and the fact that it gives him precious moments with a grandfather who will not always be near to impart wisdom and encouragement. While golf, like many sporting pleasures, largely sustains itself, there are days when having both the weather and a score over 90 is dispiriting. He tells us that on such days he receives abundant practice in the virtues of patience and self-control. We suspect that it is fortitude that gets him out of the rough.

Another common way within a family to practice fortitude is with respect to household tasks. Something always needs repair. That is the nature of machinery and this life. Now, we can adopt different attitudes when something, like a car or appliance, breaks down. We can let it ruin the rest of the day, venting our frustration and even blaming others (e.g., "I told you that car needed to go into the shop"), or we can remain reasonably calm, accepting the inconvenience, and looking for the best way to address it. Fortitude helps conquer frustration and anger, and correspondingly builds the related virtue of patience.

I confess fixing things is not my strength. As I left the house Saturday in search of the missing pliers, I not-so-whimsically remarked to my wife that I was off on another mission of "search and destroy." This is not my intent, of course, but seems to be the end result as the screws disappear into the grass, the door continues to drag on the floor, and I've applied the last band-aid to my cut fingers. I have consciously tried to enhance my patience in the face of these household dilemmas. Most helpful in this respect has been watching a far more skillful neighbor set projects aside, saying, "I better stop for a while or I'll make a mess of it." This may not seem like much to you, but it was revelation to me. Even knowledgeable craftsman I learned cool down, step back to get a relaxed perspective, when the going gets tough. This is fortitude at work. Not pressing ahead to finish in a sloppy or incomplete manner, but not giving up either. One aspiration I have for myself as parent is to cultivate this wisdom in my children, earlier and more completely, then I have mastered it myself. This means allowing them to try, and fail if necessary, at projects that may be beyond most children their age, and that I know I could have done myself (admittedly, a relatively small set of projects). Virtue requires practice, even when the doors aren't likely to be plumb.

Another related aspect of fortitude is sometimes expressed as magnanimity. A magnanimous person is someone at ease with himself. Neither good fortune nor tremendous adversity seems to knock him off kilter. This type of person is very quick to volunteer assistance to another and slow to request it for himself. His courage results in an admired self-reliance and stability. Neither envy nor vanity mar his attitude. A person who listens and is capable of talking with anyone—the great and the ordinary.

The description of the magnanimous person is that of a leader, a healer. My own thought is that it best describes the qualities the American people earnestly desire in a president. Can this aspect of fortitude be taught within the family? Yes, and it must, if we are to have the school principals, company presidents, bankers, clergy, lawyers, and dare I say, even congressmen who will inspire in the years ahead. The practical task here within the family is often to restrain impulses that run contrary to this virtuous attitude. For example, the tendency to be a know-it-all or to be indifferent to the views of others; to express opinions that are ill-formed or ill-timed. So too a desire for honors, rather than the quality of being honorable, or to exercise power for power's sake must be curtailed.

As a teacher, I encounter at least two types of students after they have done poorly on a difficult examination. The first student type is consumed with his grade. He demands in a rude, abrasive manner that you detail his errors. He compares his paper to others. At best, his inquiries are shallow. "What can be done to get the extra three points?" For this student, it is not a question of his personal responsibility but of assigning blame. "That question could have been stated better." "The textbook or class didn't make that clear." The second type of student, less presumptuous and less dominated by the pursuit of the grade or mere label, carefully studies his paper, redoes the analysis, and asks for comments on *his* additional thoughts on how his answers might be stronger or better reasoned in the future.

The first student is impatient; he's done with the course and will take with him only the superficial. His poor performance will be written off as a bad day or a mean instructor. The second student aspired to do better, and still does. He will persevere with courage to understand how that might be accomplished in the future. He has the fortitude to learn. Which student would you rather have: wait on you at the hardware store? fix your car? remove a tooth? build your house? write your contracts or your will? invest your savings? operate on your heart? pray for your salvation?

Family Checklist—Fortitude

1. *Draw courage from God.* Troubles beset every family. The loss of a loved one, failing health, uncertain economic times, anxiety over the proper direction of a child. Each of these things can devastate if we think we are alone. No family meets difficulty alone, however, if it walks with God daily. Families can build the courage to meet these challenges best, not merely by praying individually in the face of crisis or disappointment, but together at regular, expected times. Asking children to say the meal prayer is an ideal time to help them find the words to enlist God's strength for the family. Even the small practice of wearing a religious symbol on one's clothing can be a helpful reminder of that strength during a difficult day.

2. *Know where you're going—set realistic, personal, and family goals.* Families can more easily be thrown off-track when they don't know where the tracks are. Family members need to share with each other their most cherished personal objectives for the year, month, week, day. In our home, we have a family tradition to write down at the start of each new year our personal goals and place them in a small basket with our Christmas decorations. When the decorations are re-opened the following year, we discover how well we have encouraged each other in their work.

3. *Practice patience.* We really live in a "fast food, fast forward" world. We no longer communicate by letter, but fax. We eat serially to suit our different tastes with microwave speed or in the car in the drive-thru. We duplicate pages in books, rather than thinking about and writing notes about their contents. Slow down. Make time for family functions from meals to shopping to the repair jobs around the house. Every child doesn't have to be in multiple extracurriculars; every parent shouldn't be spread thin, trying to deliver children to these appointed places or accommodating work commitments that exceed or strain personal capacity.

Patience also means avoiding instant complaint. If things aren't going well, don't dwell on them with others. Express a positive attitude about your own prospects, and listen with interest to the concerns of others. Often, just listening to others' problems can minimize your own.

4. *Let children try.* Do less *for* children and more *with* them. Even a young child can dust or vacuum or clear dishes or put his or her own laundry in closets. At first, the tasks will not be performed to your satisfaction, but borrowing patience from item number 3, over time enough self-confidence will emerge to give children courage to assume responsibilities, even when you are not around to direct.

5. *Be courageous in defending the family.* If a textbook or a television show or a movie is antagonistic to the family, write the author or the producer or the editor or the general manager of the station. Let the source hear from you—not angrily but forthrightly. In business and personal activity, authentically make decisions that advance the family. For example, whenever possible, arrange to keep work out of the evening or weekend hours, and be courageously candid with co-workers about the reason, namely, because family is important and it relies upon your presence. Be willing to be accounted as foolish by some of the "crowd," when you make decisions that put family first.

6. *Forgive generously.* It takes tremendous fortitude to forgive, especially when no apology is offered. Be the first to reconcile after an argument, not by abandoning principle, but by finding the areas of remaining common interest. Don't indulge in talking behind someone's back. It is better to remain silent than to create obstacles to forgiveness with harsh words or demands for immediate reparation.

7. *Encourage.* Compliment those who are genuinely helping families, especially at times of need or who quietly suffer an injustice for the good of all. Write a short note to those who have been especially trustworthy or honorable in action or judgment. In conversation or public presentation, never play down to a group or an individual. Call upon the highest aspirations for yourself and help others see how much they can personally accomplish.

8. *Try to be a good citizen, especially as an example to your children.* Much of what our modern government does, or attempts to do, can be troublesome. It often takes courage to avoid being openly cynical about added layers of taxation or burdensome regulation or some other publicly inspired weight placed upon day-to-day life. It helps to remember that most public ideas (even those that seem

entirely idiotic) had some noble beginning. Children learn political cues from parents. Help them see that it is one thing to disagree with this or that policy or program, it is another to indulge in caricature. Within the family, build respect for the structure of democratic government, even if it may not be populated presently by people for whom you have individual respect.

9. *Fear openly and with maturity.* There are some frightening occurrences in life (from murder to long-term unemployment to the next calculus examination). Let children know that it is all right to express fear by responsibly expressing it yourself. The expression of fear to another often allows for imaginary evils to be set aside and the real source of worry to be identified and addressed.

10. *Do not fear death.* Obviously, this is not an invitation to act recklessly or to engage in excessively dangerous activities. It does mean accepting in the fullest possible sense that death is inevitable, and for the believer, a necessary step on a return journey to God. What's more, since we know "neither the date nor the hour," death itself is a positive reminder that today must be lived courageously, since tomorrow may or may not be ours.

Temperance

Do you not know that your bodies are members of Christ?
—St. Paul to the Corinthians 6:15–20

As a virtue, temperance is a matter of self-control, moderation. It is primarily directed at two emotions or appetites: of food and drink and for sexual activity. First off, it should be noted that there is nothing wrong or shameful about either appetite. Believers trace them both to God's wisdom and His intention that man thrive and multiply. All of us, whether possessed of great faith or not, can see these appetites as part of human nature. These are *natural* activities. That said, it is important to see that they are not ends in themselves. This is fairly obvious with eating and drinking. When we say that someone "lives to eat," it is not a compliment, but a criticism that he or she has no other source of personal fulfillment. Modern entertainment with its casual, even brazen, emphasis on "liberated" sexuality has clouded recognition of this in regard to the sexual appetite, but it is true there as well. Liberated sexuality, as it turns out, is largely using others for self-gratification and pleasure without responsibility.

If we recognize that our ingrained appetites are means to ends, then temperance becomes easy to apply once those ends are identified. With respect to eating and drinking, the desired end is quite obviously good health; with respect to sexuality, it is the total gift of self within a stable marriage relationship that is open and welcoming to the possibility of new life. When the appetites are indulged in ways (to excess) or contexts (outside marriage) that are not directed at these ends, then we have succumbed to vice, rather than advanced the formation of virtue.

Application of the virtue of temperance within a family may seem to be more consciously done already than the practice of some other virtues. Many of us always seem to be on a diet or resolving to undertake a new physical exercise regimen—at least, that is, after the 1st of the year, the next birthday, this pizza, or whatever. Unfortunately, the resolutions are difficult to keep, and sometimes, even the resolutions themselves can become their own source of vice, as when a person becomes too obsessed with physical appearance.

Excesses in food or drink, or even the more purposeless use of drugs, often result from a desire to escape work tensions or financial difficulties or just the mundane nature of day-to-day life. Here the family must help its troubled member to see the complete disconnection between, say, food consumption, and the solutions to these problems. Often this means taking the time to talk through a problem, suggesting concrete paths of action, and prayer. On occasion, needed balance can be restored by involving the family member in specific tasks or activities within the home to literally "take their mind off" the destabilizing trouble.

As a general matter, deep depression and anxiety ought not be the cause of excess in children. More likely overeating is the result of an inactive, unengaged, or unchallenged mind. In short, too little to do and no one to do it with—the situation of many so-called "home alone" or latchkey children. The temptation toward drugs can be the result of this aimlessness as well, with an added push from other undirected or misdirected "friends." If this behavior is too entrenched, families are well-advised to seek professional counseling for their child, particularly at a counseling or therapy center that shares the family's faith.

Sexual responsibility or chastity (that is, maintaining a proper sexual attitude depending upon one's status in life as unmarried, married, or celibate) depends heavily upon parental instruction and example. The evidence is overwhelming that children from so-called dysfunctional families produce them in the next generation. Divorced parents breed divorced children. Children raised outside of intact, two-parent families have greater difficulty forming lasting relationships with their own marriage partners.[8]

Sexual education within the home naturally depends on age. Pre-teen children should be taught to understand—in a very general sense—sexuality as the parents way of participating in God's creation. While children five, six, seven years of age cannot comprehend, and should not be exposed to, the details of the reproductive process, they should unashamedly know that the love Mom and Dad have for each other is good, and this love proximately accounts for their existence. A fun way to instruct in this area is to point out the particular physical features that a child has of each parent. Children really treasure hearing that they have "their mother's eyes" or "their father's strong jaw," and so forth. Creating a family tree showing pictures in a family album of who married whom conveys in a simple, personal way the contribution, continuity, and responsibility of man and wife from one generation to the next. In our family, we have given each child a family name and placed a picture of their namesake in their rooms.

As children approach the adolescent years, more specific information about responsible reproductive behavior must be conveyed by parents, usually not in one grand lecture but from time-to-time in anticipation or answer as bodily changes occur. These comments from parent to child ought not be overly scientific or mechanical, but personal. It is common to feel a bit awkward broaching the subject with a son or daughter for the first time, but parents should work to overcome that awkwardness, in order to stress how beautiful new manhood and womanhood can and should be. The body is created in God's image; it is good if used for good purposes. Awkwardness is real, and quite importantly, an outgrowth of ingrained modesty. In this, it may be useful to convey how the marriage relationship itself is the only true way to reconcile sexuality with natural modesty.

The subject of modesty with teenagers is an important one. One's state of dress, or undress, can stimulate appetite for sexual activity. This is especially true for boys, and it is a fact which requires little elaboration. As with the subject of temperance gen-

---

8   Barbara Dafoe Whitehead, "Dan Quayle Was Right," *The Atlantic Monthly* (April 1993), p. 47.

erally, whether something is appropriate dress depends on whether it is directed at an appropriate end. For a husband and wife committed to each other and open to the responsibility of parenthood, the use of dress to enhance their sexual attractiveness to one another is entirely proper. These matters are respected and private. Yet, the same forms of dress would be entirely improper between an unmarried couple, since as a means, it would be directed at an entirely unacceptable object: sexual relations outside of marriage.

In discussing the virtue of temperance, as with all virtues, we recognize that there are corresponding vices. To allow children to dress immodestly is to court the risks and dangers of that vice, namely, the misuse of sexual appetite to occasion adultery and fornication, and the sadness of the soul and the human despondency that results when pleasure is sought for pleasure's sake. An uncontrolled desire for pleasure cannot be satisfied. It is an irrational passion that leads, in its worst forms, to spouse abuse and rape. The most practical advice for families on this score is to not hide or understate the need to control this passion. Parents would do well to pass on precisely the words of St. Paul to their children: "Flee immorality. Every sin that a man commits is outside the body, but the immoral man sins against his own body."[9] The modern translation? Flee MTV and everything it portrays and represents.

There are many other aspects to temperance. Part of this great virtue underscores the need for kindness in our dealings with others. For the family, kindness means cultivating a disposition of forgiveness, rather than vengeance, when wrongs have been done to us. Holding our tongue, when others go out of their way to provoke us. To judge properly, but not harshly, the actions of others. Opposed to or corrosive of kindness within the family is anger. On any given day, we all may have a "short fuse." The task for husband and wife is to encourage each other to identify, and then avoid, those little things—and they usually are quite little things—which provoke us. In other words, a real help here is for members of the family to be encouraged not to brood over, but disclose, the source of anger. This does not mean pointing to someone in an accusatory way but, rather, confessing frustration and pleading thereby for a family shoulder upon which to be comforted.

---

9   I Cor. 6: 15-20.

Humility too is part of temperance. Here the task is to avoid self-promotion and pride. The best way to do this within the family is to ask sincerely about another's day. In other words, to learn to listen and listen carefully and to be quite reticent to talk about oneself. Strengthening humility also helps us get past anger, by inclining us to better understand our own shortcomings.

It would be possible to go on in this vein, seeing for example, the daily encouragement of a child's commitment to study and learning as an aspect of temperance. Such dedication, like the pursuit of virtuous habits generally, manifests a desire for wisdom. When a family undertakes to help its children learn little by little to reason from what is already known, to speak calmly and honestly, to walk gracefully, to show sincere interest in others and things of beauty, or to master a skill, that family demonstrates its commitment to the pursuit of personal virtue. And this family commitment reveals an understanding that the formation of good character involves both faith and hard work, and that the former requires a great deal of the latter.

Family Checklist—Temperance

1. *Understand food, drink, and sexual activity as means to proper ends.* The proper end of food and drink is respect for the functions of the body and good health; for sexual activity the end must always be as an expression of total commitment to spouse and children within marriage.

2. *Relate sexual responsibility to the personal generations of your family.* Demonstrate the chain of responsible sexual activity that leads to each child. For example, help children understand through family albums and stories how their traits and features are the culmination of committed married lives of ancestors gone before.

3. *Teach sexual responsibility day-to-day.* Don't rely upon teachers or federal programs. As bodily changes occur, help children understand their naturalness, and how these changes call for self-restraint in ways they previously did not confront.

4. *Encourage modest or appropriate dress.* Part of self-control is directing sexual activity to the privacy of a marriage relationship. Immodest dress and action is a manifestation of a lack of understanding or respect for the proper end of sexual activity. It is indeed a public invitation to the improper.

5. *Flee MTV.* By this it is meant that we should avoid modern invitations to immorality as much as possible. Admit to children

that we are all tempted to overindulge in food or enticed by sexually explicit displays. The virtue of temperance is helped, not hindered, when cable isn't pumping temptation into the living room twenty-four hours per day.

6. *Judge the transgressions of others with kindness.* Anger is in direct opposition to temperance. We must consciously work to lengthen our personal "fuses." In young children, it helps to admonish the wrongfulness of anger as it occurs. With ourselves, the habit of virtue is advanced by keeping still or admitting anger in non-specific, non-confrontational ways. For example, telling a spouse: "I'm really angry about this now, let's talk later." Time is a great healer, and it often allows us to see the source of anger—later at least—as trivial. If anger is proper at all, it is as a controlled means of correcting improper behavior.

7. *Be humble.* It is intemperate to trumpet your own skills and achievements. Inquire about the work of others before discussing your own. Be genuinely happy about another's good fortune. When something has gone wrong, and it is all or partially your fault, honestly admit that fault without casting blame on others.

8. *Strive for balance.* Family and outside work are in competition. It is responsible to seek a good income for one's family; it is irresponsible to allow that pursuit of income to displace family and family time.

9. *Learn for the sake of learning.* This is so very easy in young children, yet so easily forfeited. A young child's curiosity is immense, and parents must strive to avoid minimizing that desire to learn with an undue emphasis on grades or by demonstrating a lack of interest or annoyance with a child's many interests. In our own lives, we must resist laziness or complacency. Legitimate ambition and an appreciation for mastering the details of new projects, books, skills sets the best course and example.

10. *Seek moderation.* Every activity from work to speech to dress has a right order to it. There is a Gary Larson "Far Side" cartoon that sums this up well with a somewhat bedeviled figure sitting on the edge of bed at early morning, with the caption "first pants, then shoes." Overly simple? Perhaps. But temperance does direct us to be neither too loud, nor too showy, nor inconsiderate of local custom, or to be overindulgent in food or recreations such as gambling. The profitability of off-track betting and state lotteries signals a greater need to pursue the moderate course.

Chapter 8
The Family and the Pursuit of Justice

You shall not be partial to the poor or defer to the great,
but in righteousness shall you judge your neighbor.
—Leviticus 19:15

UNLIKE PRUDENCE, which is a habit of the *mind*, or temperance, which is aimed at the control of *emotion*, the virtue of justice is directed at controlling our actions or *will*, as they affect either God or others. Justice thus may be divided into two large classes, that which is due God and that owed to man. The nonbeliever by definition will deny any obligation to God, but it is discussed here first, both because of the prevalence of religious belief and because to believers the two justice obligations are related by virtue of man's creation in God's image. Justice owed God is termed the virtue of religion. What is owed to man as a matter of justice is described as the giving over of that which belongs to another.

Justice Due God

For the believer, justice toward God is a recognition of the honor and reverence due the source of existence. Not surprisingly, much religious writing about justice relates to worship. Derived from the Latin word, *religando*, meaning to "bind back," the nature of religious obligation is best summarized in the first three of the Ten Commandments, which set out the recognition due the one true God and the disavowal of idols, the proper use of God's name, and the injunction to worship God in an open and public manner, unashamedly.

Prayer

Hypocrisy is unbecoming in any matter; it is despised in worship. Prayer, as a matter of justice to God, necessarily must be sincere. In families, the recitation of familiar and formal prayers, such as the "Our Father," serves to directly connect a family with the religious tradition, but the words must be understood as well as recited. Do the words "Thy will be done on earth as it is in heaven," really mean that we have placed our ultimate destiny within the will of God, not our own? We think we know what is good for us, but as the expression "be careful, sometimes you get what you ask for" reveals, that is not always true.

From the standpoint of sincerity, it is often good if family members forego formal or standard prayers at meals, and put their devotions into their own more natural or conversational terms. And because the justice owed God is not a matter of secrecy or embarrassment, there is no reason to keep prayer within the house; a prayer—not in a showy or ingenuine manner—when eating out is equally appropriate.

Placing faith in God is not only right in terms of what is owed to God, but it is also the only means to be at peace after human efforts are exhausted. As I mentioned earlier, a few years back, we lost a family member to a murder at gunpoint in an apparent robbery at work. Statistics say this is another by-product of the culture war. The entire family was dumbfounded, crushed. As we bid our slain loved one goodbye, his father, a gentle man, said simply: "At some point, children are on their own." It was a sad, but not hopeless, lament since it was said in a spirit of earnest trust in God. None there wanted to lose our brother, and nothing on earth, then or now, eases the pain of his loss. Yet, while no one understood the reason for his untimely death, all there understood and accepted that when God entered his name into the Book of Life, He knew both dates. As God is the source of goodness, it was now up to us to let "Thy will be done." It is only in this acceptance, I am convinced, that a family ever moves beyond grief.

Church Services

Keeping the Lord's Day is likewise commanded in the Decalogue. We are obligated to this with gratitude, respect, and constancy. Respect is easily manifested by proper dress and behavior. Unfortunately, today some parents neglect these features in themselves and require even less of their children. Laughing and talking during church services, reading books unrelated to the service, or showing up late or in the same outfit that one changes the oil in the car is unjustified.

The observance of the Sabbath traditionally meant setting aside as well one's normal, occupational duties. In modern America, many of us either continue to do normal work in the office or at home via computer. Even when work is foregone, the substitutes (going to the mall or watching television) hardly manifest special recognition of lives owed to a Divine Creator.

If justice to God is to be taken seriously, the organization of life within the family must reflect it. With a little imagination, it is easy to design family traditions that can signify the special nature of the Sabbath. Perhaps, it might be as simple as using the formal dinnerware or eating in the dining room rather than the kitchen. Under the best of circumstances, it would mean undertaking activities that connect family members personally with one another. Building a model plane, playing baseball, taking a long family walk, visiting an elderly relative or friend, or helping a neighbor might all more justly give God His due by showing care and respect for those, like us, made in His image.

Justice toward One Another

What do we owe to others? Asking the question we see immediately that as a matter of virtue, justice relates to duty, obligation. In modern America, the self-centered attitude of "getting justice," as in demanding one's rights, is quite opposite. That justice is presently misunderstood in a highly individualistic way as a sophisticated kind of "tit for tat" vengeance highlights again the ill-consequence of separating education and religion. It is from religion that we are instructed in matters of faith, hope, and, especially in this context, charity. The administration of justice without a good understanding of charity makes justice legalistic and unfeeling—unable to grasp not only the subtleties of particular cases but also why some wrongs are more properly a matter of forgiveness than rectification.

That said, the virtue justice must not be collapsed into charity because that confusion in itself gives rise to specious claims of "right." For example, as a matter of *distributive* justice (more on this term shortly), we have an obligation to see that *common or public* goods are distributed proportionately and fairly among all citizens. Thus, when the state creates, as it already has, a public fund for education, it is a violation of distributive justice to exclude parents with children in religious schools from sharing in that fund. By contrast, where the policy or community decision has not yet been made to create a public or common fund, it is not a violation of distributive justice to argue against its creation. Take universal health care as an example. The president's call for this is a matter of charity, not justice. And as a matter of charity, it is best handled below within the smaller sovereigns of family, church congregation, and especially religious hospitals. Overlooking the distinction between justice and charity understates the moral difficulty of inviting the national government to displace families in matters of personal health. The president's call for nationalized health care was, I believe, largely rejected on these (and of course the related economic) grounds. But just as it was wrong to say that there was a *"right* to health care," as a matter of justice, so too it would be wrongful for the smaller sovereigns to now disregard their individual health-care obligations to parents, children, employees, and parishioners that originate in charity. Charity opens the heart and builds community; a premature or unwarranted claim of justice erects a government bureaucracy and deadens man's relationship with man.

Justice, and its sibling equality, is said to involve a number of elements: others, an obligation, and the observance of the obligation strictly. In other words, justice and the derivative idea of equality are workable only if there is a reasonably clear specification of what is owed to others; that is, what our obligations are and, correlatively, what others may then claim as a matter of right. While philosophers can wander all over the lot with this type of question, for families in need of a concrete answer, I submit, there are really only two possible sources of obligation: God or man. Tracing obligation to God means locating duty in His revealed teaching or in the human nature that God has given each of us. In other words, the two "mega-virtues" discussed in earlier chapters. When obligations (and correlative rights) flow from God and human nature, the list is quite manageable and fixed over time to include, for example, life and physical integrity, liberty, property, marriage, religious worship, reputation, education, and responsible inquiry and expression.[1] Obligations derived from man are

---

1   The list is variously stated, but it usually approximates those listed in the text. See generally, Jacques Maritain, *The Rights of Man and Natural Law*, trans. Doric C. Anson (New York: Charles Scribner's

almost entirely specifications of these obligations fixed by God and the human nature of His creation. Because that is so, man-made obligations and rights can *add*, but as a matter of moral justice, *not subtract from*, the obligations or rights that are derived from God— or in the felicitous words of the Declaration of Independence, "the Law of Nature and Nature's God."

The virtue of justice is frequently divided into three sub-categories: legal, distributive, and commutative. The first, legal justice, deals with an individual's responsibility to the community; distributive justice, as already briefly mentioned, is the converse—that is, the community's obligations to the individual; and commutative justice deals with our obligations to one another. Let's briefly look at each sub-category in turn and what they specifically mean for the family. But remember, each sub-category is ultimately traceable to an obligation derived from either God or man, and the latter must never presume the capacity to displace the former.

Legal Justice—Duties of Individual to Community

Legal justice is primarily the obligation to support the common good. As a concept, that is indeed vague, but its significance to the family is this teaching: *We do not live alone.* Instead, we live in community, and we must be connected to it. So, how do we connect? First, by preparing ourselves and our children to treat others with respect, honesty, and deference. Second, by learning a trade or gaining knowledge that can be put to use in the community. Third, by not causing harm, or if harm is caused, by rectifying it as fully as possible. It is important to understand two features of these requirements as a family. The common good means that no matter how "autonomous" or self-sufficient we think we may be—with our professional degrees or modern appliances or computerized "windows"—we are not hermits or isolationists. In this sense, the individual does not stand apart from the community but is *in* it and has responsibility for and to it. Yet, the emphasis on community does not mean that individual welfare is sacrificed for the good of the greatest number. Rather, the common good is advanced only when individual good is also. For example, our use of property may be limited in proportionate ways to achieve an

---

Sons, 1943), p. 65, and Charles Sheedy, *The Christian Virtues*, 2d ed. (Notre Dame, Ind.: University of Notre Dame Press, 1951), p. 177, citing a work by Msgr. John A. Ryan.

overall good. While such limitation may seem in isolation to curtail individual good, in fact, if the regulation is well-drawn to prevent harm, it actually advances individual good both by the protection it bestows on all and the need for rectification of harm that it avoids.

Claims of legal justice can range from that involving risk of life and limb to that easily fulfilled. One of the most difficult claims of legal justice for a family concerns military duty. Giving up family responsibilities to serve one's country seems clearly to favor the common good over that of individual good. Yet, as with the property-regulation example above, time given to military service secures both individual and common good, as the community obligation of military service is the proximate guarantor of the well being of both individual and family. The sacrifices made by men and women in uniform, especially, of course, the "ultimate" sacrifice, are virtuous acts of humility and respect for legal justice. Throughout our nation's history, this has been expressed many times, but consider two moving expressions which capture the bittersweet interconnectedness of duty to country and family sacrifice. The first is that of Sullivan Ballou, who left his law practice, wife, and two sons to join the Union Army in the Civil War. On the eve of the Battle of Bull Run, he wrote his wife:

> I feel impelled to write a few lines that may fall under your eye when I am no more. . . . "Not my will, but Thine, O God, be done." If it is necessary that I should fall on the battlefield for my country, I am ready. I have no misgivings about, or lack of confidence in the cause in which I am engaged. And my courage does not falter. I know how American civilization now bears upon the triumph of the Government, and how great a debt we owe to those who went before us through blood and suffering of the Revolution. And I am willing—perfectly willing to lay down all my joys in this life to help maintain this government and to pay that debt.
>
> Sarah, my love for you is deathless. It seems to bind me with mighty cables that nothing but omnipotence can break. And yet my love of country comes over me like a strong wind and bears me irresistibly to the battlefield. The memories of the blissful moments I have enjoyed with you come crowding over me, . . . and how hard it is for me to give them up! And burn to ashes the hopes of future years when God willing we might still have loved and loved together and seen our boys grow up to honorable manhood around us. I know I have few claims upon Divine Providence but something whispers to

me—perhaps it is my little Edgar—that I should return to my loved ones unharmed. . . ."[2]

One week later, Sullivan Ballou died of injuries sustained by cannon fire in the Battle of Bull Run.

A second expression of military duty as legal justice is a more contemporary letter. Carmen Gordon explains to her two young children, Ian and Brittany, the death of their father, Master Sergeant Gary Gordon, who gave his life trying to rescue a fellow soldier in Mogadishu, Somalia, in 1993. Mrs. Gordon writes:

> You will read what the president of the United States said when he awarded the Medal of Honor: "Gary Gordon . . . died in the most courageous and selfless way any human being can act." But you may still ask why. You may ask how he could have been devoted to two families so equally, dying for one but leaving the other.
>
> For your father, there were no hard choices in life. Once he committed to something, the way was clear. He chose to be a husband and father, and never wavered in those roles. He chose the military, and "I shall not fail those with whom I serve" became his simple religion. When his other family needed him, he did not hesitate, as he would not have hesitated for us.[3]

Voting too is a claim of legal justice. One that puts us in far less physical danger than the military service Sullivan Ballou and Sergeant Gordon rendered so fully. In truth, voting requires very little of us. Yet, legal justice demands it as obligation. In times past, the failure to exercise this duty was said to be a grave sin or injustice, especially if the office at stake was of considerable consequence.[4] Obviously, in light of the ever smaller percentage of individuals presently exercising the franchise, this understanding has waned considerably. What practically can be done? It's easy. Take the little ones and show them the inside of the booth next time you have an opportunity to vote. They'll remember, and you will have accom-

---

2   "Letter from a Soldier" in *Themes in Literature*, ed. Jan Anderson (Pensacola, Fla.: A Beka Book, 1991), p. 118.

3   "Letters to Our Children," *U.S. News & World Report* (August 1, 1994), p. 33.

4   See, Sheedy, *supra*, p. 195.

plished a small, but important, part of the duty demanded by legal justice.

Distributive Justice—What the Community Owes the Individual

We have already introduced this subject in the mention of the injustice that presently exists in the selective access to the public fund for education, excluding students attending religious schools. But the principle applies to all public funds or public property: the government must distribute these without favoritism or improper discrimination. So too the principle can rightly be relied upon as a prohibition against vote fraud or public corruption, where public office is obtained or asserted illegitimately or its benefits used personally. That seems obvious, but in the wake of Iran-Contra and Whitewater, it deserves special mention.

Distributive justice requires that taxes raised by the government be directed at legitimate public need and that, if progressive taxation is adopted, it not reach confiscatory levels or be aimed purely at the redistribution of wealth. With monies raised, *the primary duty of the government is to ensure peace and public order*. The government is not to displace the individual or the family in local community. Indeed, quite the opposite, the government at all levels is to refrain as a matter of justice from undertaking any function that can more fitly be accomplished within the family. The government's duty is to empower or enhance the authority of the smaller sovereigns by preserving domestic order, maintaining a stable economy, and safeguarding against external threat. Beyond this, *society and culture* must be permitted to flourish with as little legal or governmental interference as possible. America in the 1990s has inverted this understanding to her detriment.

Commutative Justice—What We Owe Each Other

Commutative justice requires that we give to other persons their due. Again, however, the definition of obligation is critical to understanding this aspect of virtue. Generally speaking, we are obligated to other persons in one of two ways: first, by agreement, as in a contractual relationship; and second, as a matter of human nature.

Lawyers supply a technical, legal definition of contract—an offer, followed by acceptance, in exchange for something of value or consideration. Similarly, statutes may require that contracts be in writing to be enforceable or that they be signed by certain corporate officers before they can be considered *legally* binding. But remember, law is not morality. The virtue of justice may require that obligations be fulfilled, even when they are unenforceable under law.[5] This shouldn't be surprising, as we still speak positively of a man or woman who can "do business on a handshake" or someone "whose word is his bond."

Family promises too are not as a rule "legally" binding. A few children have been allowed to sue their parents directly in a court of law for extreme neglect, but that is a rare and entirely different matter. No, keeping promises within a family is a matter of moral respect, and it is one of the best ways to instill this virtuous habit. For example, being on time is one means for this to be demonstrated, but I will confess that this is a real struggle for me. So much so that I have taken to setting my watch eight minutes fast. (I told my son that ten minutes would be overdoing it, and five would be too little—notice, here too I am searching for the golden mean! My dear wife has suggested that my tombstone epitaph read: "I still have eight minutes." Very funny.) The point is, even though I have been living on this accelerated schedule for some time now, my entire family still regards me as a time-scofflaw. It is very hard to win a virtuous reputation back.

You probably can think of a few of your own family promises that are difficult to keep. For example, perhaps you've promised to help someone else at an awkward time, or, even more irrationally, agreed to attend their daughter's dance recital. This can surely test virtuous mettle, especially when fulfilling the obligation occurs, as it inevitably does, at the busiest point of the busiest day. Nevertheless, watching a six year old in a tutu flop about the stage can be morally instructive to other family members, even as it is excruciatingly painful to oneself.

Don't over-promise, either. A frustrating part of modern life is dealing with businesses that over-promise and then fail to deliver. Anyone who has ever built a house or added a home improvement knows of what I speak. If the work can only reasonably be accomplished in three months, it should not be promised in one. Avoid

---

5   See generally, Thomas L. Shaffer and Robert F. Cochran, Jr., *Lawyers, Clients and Moral Responsibility* (St. Paul, Minn.: West Publishing, 1994), pp. 64–65.

over-promising in a family too. We cannot always attend every little league game, and it is better to say that honestly than to promise and fail.

Marriage, of course, has traditionally involved some very solemn promises. Marital promises have some legal consequence even today, but as those men and women who have gone through the anguish of divorce know well, the law is a shallow source of virtue. The frequency of divorce suggests plainly that a vow of "until death do us part" may today express the same level of commitment as the recital of "In God We Trust" on a quarter. The disregard of the promise of lifelong marital fidelity is damaging to the children,[6] disruptive of school and community, and personally tragic.

The saga of O. J. Simpson and his murdered wife Nicole may well illustrate. While the popular press used the seemingly endless Simpson trial to focus needed attention on spouse abuse, it uniformly failed to reveal how the spouses in that union abused each other, long before Nicole suffered facial bruises or was found lifeless on her doorstep. As the widely reported facts would have it, O. J. forfeited his marital vow to his first wife by moving in with Nicole. Nicole responded in kind by divorcing O. J. a few years later. Divorce in a civil court, however, could not fully erase their union, even as shaky and tenuous as it was. Nicole was attracted toward reconciliation much to the consternation and confusion of her highly paid psychoanalysts. O. J. apparently could not stop thinking of Nicole as part of himself—perhaps in a distorted version of the Biblical sense of the "two as one." He flew into a rage upon seeing her in the embrace of another man, expressing expletive-deleted, but seemingly genuine, concern for the effect the exhibition of this would have on *their* children. In the end, O. J. wrote that his fault may have been "that he loved her too much." Yet, through the lens of commutative justice, neither of them may have loved each other enough.

Along with marriage, the love or obligation owed to parents is appropriately mentioned here. This too is an obligation derived from justice. Out of justice, there is the reciprocal obligation of love between parent and child. This love depends originally upon the close physical tie and the affirmation of cooperation with God in the creation of life. But as a practical matter, this reciprocal love must be revealed each day, if the moral duty is to be fulfilled.

---

6   See Whitehead, "Dan Quayle Was Right," pp. 50, 59–60.

On the child's side, this love is affirmed through actions of respect: not causing parents needless worry or anxiety, keeping good company, observing house rules or curfews, doing family chores and making reasonable efforts consistent with ability in school work. The matter of allowance and monetary reward is sure to come up within families. While there is no absolute rule on the subject, my own view is that the virtue of justice is better served without these payments. Granting allowances confuses what is owed out of filial love—as a matter of moral justice—with what is owed as a matter of negotiation. It is better to be financially responsive to children as needs arise and to be as generous as the circumstances of the family permit, rather than to introduce an artificial marketplace environment into the family. Put succinctly, moral formation is diluted when one has to be paid to be good.

The nature of a child's obligation to love his or her parents changes with age. As a matter of population, America is getting older. This will soon present many children in their 30s and 40s with a duty, originating out of justice, to be personally and financially helpful to their elderly parents. This is apparently a worldwide phenomenon, as recently a member of the Singapore parliament introduced legislation to require sons and daughters under law to provide for their parents.[7] The author of this proposal partially recognized that "[t]he law cannot legislate love between parents and children or husbands and wives." Nevertheless, he advocated the law's involvement as a "safety net."

This is well-intentioned but misguided. Creating a cause of action for damages when children fail to provide for their parents will result in substituting the law's requirements for moral duty. Faced with legal penalty, many children will not long remember that they are aiding their elderly fathers and mothers out of justice. Moreover, with the law in place, too many children will think their duty discharged upon payment of the amount of assistance the law demands. If cases of neglect of parents are widespread, the first corrective must come from within the family itself, or the church, in the form of directly—even bluntly and publicly—instructing moral delinquents of their duty.

When governments get involved in family matters, they must respect families. Assistance must be rendered without harm or the

---

7   Walter Woon, "Honor Thy Father and Mother—Or Else," *Wall Street Journal* (June 28, 1994), p. A18.

limitation of family discretion. With reference to helping children provide financially for elderly parents, the government might consider lessening the tax bite on children. In the health-care debate, for example, I suggested that children who purchased insurance for their parents might be given a tax credit. Again, filial piety—as love of parents is called—should not depend upon such economic boost, but today when the government consumes an overly large share of a family's income, this might be chalked up as a small effort to bring things back into proper balance.

Children, of course, have a duty to obey their parents in all lawful matters. The duty of obedience extends to teachers, who stand in the place of parents during the school day. The obligation of obedience includes adult children as well if they continue to live within the parents' household. This is unfortunately an increasing occurrence as graduates encounter difficulty finding jobs directly following school or as children return home following failed marriages.

To foster obedience, it must be insisted upon early and firmly, but not meanly. The sooner in a child's life this is implemented the better, as issuing commands to undisciplined adolescents who can no longer be carried off to bed is problematic. Obviously, as a child approaches or enters adulthood, there is more reason to explain the need to follow one course rather than another. Such explanation may actually benefit a parent. For example, not infrequently when I make manly, but not always successful, efforts to repair our tractor, I will instruct my son rather specifically, only to be alerted by Mr. Smarty-Pants that there is an easier way.

On a parent's side, justice requires that children be loved in matters relating to this world and the next. Children can get under foot, especially after a difficult day at work or in the home. Not surprisingly, a recent University of Illinois study reveals that the manner in which children are treated by fathers reflects the way in which Dad was treated that day on the job.[8] Such research obviously contains a message for employers about their responsibility to assist in family stability, but it should not obscure that out of justice, parents must learn to treat their children with warmth and respect, even when all is not well down at the shop.

Perhaps the most important and specific duty of a parent is to

---

8   Sue Shellenbarger, "Dad Takes Home a Tough Day at Work," *Wall Street Journal* (June 29, 1994), p. B1.

see to a child's proper education—physically, intellectually and spiritually. Too many American children are out-of-shape "couch potatoes," suggesting that parents are not instructing children properly in terms of diet or fitness. Children need meals at regular hours, household duties, and exercise. The matter of schooling has already been discussed extensively in Chapter 7. However, it is worth underscoring that it is moral justice which requires that a child's intellectual and spiritual instruction be comprehensive and, whenever possible, proceed together and harmoniously. On a practical level, this will frequently mean enrolling children in a religious school if one in the family's faith tradition is available. But even more critically, it means linking life and faith through frequent family discussion. My wife and I have found that a comfortable time to fulfill this obligation is after Sunday service at dinner. Asking the younger children to re-tell the Scripture reading in their own words can be quite revealing. It indicates not only their own precious and delightfully innocent insights but also how well or poorly the instruction actually was. Asking older children how religious instruction applies to events in their own lives is a fruitful way to prevent such instruction from remaining abstract or distant. In addition, when children know that they may be asked about church instruction, the level of attention given by them in church itself improves.

Thus far, we have been discussing commutative justice as it originates from contract or promise, including the special promises implicit in marriage and in the assumption of parenthood. The latter obligations serve as a good bridge to the obligations of commutative justice that flow from human nature itself. As will be seen, these often relate to one of three subjects: bodily integrity, property, or reputation.

Bodily Integrity

Under this heading, abortion, suicide, murder, euthanasia are all proscribed. Why? St. Paul gives what I believe is the only sufficient answer: "We do not own ourselves." Life is a gift, and as a gift, we do not fulfill the obligations associated with it if we forfeit it in these ways.

The gravest assault upon this principle of commutative justice comes from the modern claim that we are "unowned" or have an absolute "right to be let alone," or the right "to define our own concept of existence," as if we were our own creator This view has been popularized by the Supreme Court,[9] and it originates out of an extreme and mistaken view of individual liberty. After hours of interesting, but fruitless, academic discussion, these sweeping claims of radical individualism can, in my judgment, be answered only out of the mega-virtues of belief in God and a knowable truth.

To be sure, scientific evidence can be gathered to show each unborn child as genetically unique and complete from the moment of fertilization. So too suicide can be argued to deprive society of a person's singular and valuable contribution or to be caused by severe depression that is temporary and conquerable. Euthanasia can be shown to lead to a lack of credibility in the medical profession and, even more fundamentally, to be unnecessary in light of modern pain-killers, hospice care, and their ethical administration. Murder can be declared a "capital crime." In their way, each of these arguments or deterrents against departing from the bodily integrity aspect of commutative justice is significant, but they remain secondary to the fact that in taking life, we are taking that which we do not own.

How then can families instill the principle of bodily integrity? The most obvious way is through affirmation of faith in God's ownership of us. This positive faith must stand in constant rebuttal of the modern disregard of this principle. A disregard that is re-told on the evening news in the sound-bite summation of assisted suicides, drive-by killings, sexual assaults, and abortion activities. Children hear and see these tragedies in graphic detail, and parents cannot pretend otherwise. Rather, these appalling times cry out for age-sensitive instruction from parent to child that there can never be a necessity or liberty to do wrong. False claims of freedom are merely claims of license to be irresponsible. Relatedly, as children mature, parents must direct them toward their own proper family and married lives. And when parents speak up, they are heard. Empirically, for example, parents have proven to be the best educators of chastity or, in contemporary vocabulary, sexual responsibility.[10]

Watching my wife run a pre-school for three, four, and five year

---

9   *Planned Parenthood v. Casey*, 112 S. Ct. 2791, 2807 (1992), affirming *Roe v. Wade*; 410 U.S. 959 (1973).

10   Stephen A. Small and Tom Luster, "Adolescent Sexual Activity: An Ecological Risk-Factor Approach," *Journal of Marriage and Family* 56 (1994), pp. 181–92.

olds and observing my own five children, I also know that at an early age, parents may see children push or bully another into yielding a toy or some other object. This intrusion on bodily integrity may be passed off as, "Oh, they don't know any better." True, they may not, but moral formation begins *now*. Disregard for the well being of others and the selfishness it manifests must be resisted and fairly disciplined then and there, as its claims merely grow in magnitude.

Property

The virtue of commutative justice affirms the right of private property. In so doing, it condemns theft and requires that any such theft be rectified. Disputes about the moral justification for private property are as old as the world itself. Yet, this much is apparent: Man did not create and, therefore, has no initial claim to the earth and all its material resources. That said, the connection between a person's development and property is so close that private ownership is seen as a rational extension of bodily integrity. Owning property creates personal initiative and safeguards the family in terms of shelter. It also allows the maintenance of reserves or funds for the long-term development and needs of family members, with respect to education, health care, and retirement. In addition, a well-defined and settled private property system safeguards public order and peace (and through these conditions) the pursuit of all of the basic, cardinal virtues.

Private property is essential to a family's ability to provide for itself. These needs are best met by the family because they are best known there, and any other means of distribution requires a political bureaucracy that harms genuine freedom. Without private property, we would be mired in endless disputes over who has what degree of access to things, and the frequency of these disputes would threaten life itself.

Even when disputes would not directly threaten bodily integrity, holding resources in common with no one person having sufficient incentive to care for them has been shown to lead not to careful conservation but aggressive consumption.[11] The most polluted, least cared for, environmental resources are air and water,

---

11   Hardin, "The Tragedy of the Commons," *Science*, 162 (1968), pp. 1244–45; Demsetz, "Toward a Theory of Property Rights," *American Economic Review*, 57 (1967), pp. 347–57.

and they are owned in common. Compare the last time you planted flowers in the public park with the garden in your yard.

Private property is thus a sound second principle. It is the best system capable of being devised in an imperfect world. It is not an unqualified right, as private property ought not be used in an abusive way in disregard of private necessity or the reasonable demands of the common good or the theological virtue of charity that calls upon each of us to use any surplus for the good of others. Believers find this summation of virtue as it relates to property in the Gospel. In Christ's discussion with the rich young man, He first reminds him of the commandment, "Thou shall not steal," affirming the importance of private ownership. But, says Christ, "If you have in mind to be perfect, then sell what you have and follow me."[12] In short, the justice of private property can lead to good in the here and now, but it ought not distract us from our ultimate end. "Seek first the kingdom of God and His justice, and all these things shall be given you besides."[13]

What does this mean for the instruction of virtue within families? First, parents must respect the goods of others. When a tool or article of clothing is borrowed, it must be returned promptly and in good shape. Second, these same habits must be practiced with the children. Children are notorious "borrowers," formally from the library and informally from their siblings and friends. (I'm still looking for my blue-striped shirt in the closet, and I've noticed that my black shoes tend to leave the house in the morning before I do.) Good habits begin with books being returned on or before the due date and long-sleeve shirts, shoes, or the family car leaving only with permission and returning intact.

So too respecting the privacy of neighbors in the use of their yards and home should be encouraged. Children can easily avoid taking short cuts through private property or sledding or playing basketball or baseball where they have not been invited. The neighbor may well have a fine lawn for practicing chip shots, but permission is a necessary first. And if permission is denied, respect for property advises polite acceptance of that refusal, not rude resentment.

Reviewing what justice requires in terms of property with teenagers can make a real difference in attitude. Teenagers love to stay

---

12   Matthew 19:16–26; Luke 18:18–23.

13   Matthew 6:19–21,33.

over at another's home. Yet, these "stay overs" ought not be understood as occasions for leaving virtuous behavior behind. "Thou shalt not steal," applies equally well whether the potato chips are on the shelf at the grocery or in the pantry of a friend's kitchen. Parents understand the voracious appetites of teens, and many will have no objection to (or as a matter of charity will tolerate) their foodstuffs disappearing, but every parent I know has respect only for the visiting friend who asks first.

Teens also like to declare "ownership" of parts of the household when they visit. A similar acquisitiveness exists on public buses with blaring boomboxes or while riding in an open car giving everyone within blocks the "benefit" of their choice of music. These are indicators of unkind behavior, but at their moral root, they are injustices stemming from a disregard of the peace and order that is entailed by respect for property. To be sure, many of these slights to justice may be characterized as small matters, but they are cumulative and they all "count" in the formation of character.

Parents can also demonstrate respect for property, and aid the formation of that respect in their children, by promptly correcting economic errors that run in their favor; for example, when they are undercharged for goods or services received at a store. Similarly, refraining from equipping the household with the pens, pencils, and materials from the office instills an attitude of honesty in children even in those circumstances when we are "unwatched" by all—except God, of course.

Finally, lapses from moral behavior do occur. When they do— that is, when parents or children willfully disregard the property of others—the virtue of commutative justice, demands proportionate and prompt restitution. The less effort there is to hide behind technicalities—e.g., "I wasn't the one who opened the chips," the more likely it is that the path to virtue is being followed.

Reputation

This aspect of the virtue of commutative justice goes to the very heart of civility. The moral obligation included under this subheading includes avoiding the premature judgment of others, constantly engaging in detraction or talking behind the back of others, and ridiculing or insulting a person in their presence.

Believers know that Christ cautions: "Judge not, that you may not be judged."[14] However, it is all too easy for us to fall into the habit of sizing one another up quickly, often too quickly. We may even judge by appearances or manner of speech or dress. In life, we may be called upon to judge or evaluate others. Jury duty is an example and so is serving on your office's hiring committee. There is nothing wrong with exercising these functions, even expeditiously, so long as the record of the person or the account of his past actions is fully understood in regard to the purpose of the evaluation. Injustice occurs, however, when we use superficial criteria to ascribe deficiency or bad behavior to another.

In the family, this type of rash judgment can sometimes be heard among children. "You're *always* taking my things." "You *never* do what you are supposed to do." And so forth. These sweeping condemnations do not do justice to the person condemned, and we know it almost as quickly as we utter the statement. The practice of hesitating, "biting one's tongue," as it were, is what is called for to stop the utterance beforehand.

A similar, but more serious, vice is demeaning others out of their presence. This is really a form of slander, although again not in the sense of the law but of morality. The law makes truth a defense to both slander and the detraction in written form, called libel. But the moral obligation of justice draws no distinction based on truth because the harm is in the theft of reputation, not the level of veracity in the remark. Here, I am reminded again of the tragic O. J. Simpson case. Many people were heard to complain after Mr. Simpson was charged with his wife's murder—"How come we weren't told earlier that he was a wife-beater?" If the only purpose in knowing this information, however, would have been to run Mr. Simpson's more favorable public reputation into the ground, it would have constituted an unjust purpose. In this regard, we should not overlook that even if a person is not fully entitled to a positive public reputation, the mere fact of this reputation can act as an encouragement to do good or the right thing.

It is natural at the end of the day to return home, and in the evening, get together with friends or neighbors to "chew the fat." If "the fat," however, consists entirely of gossiping about how so-and-so is a poor mother or poor father or poor employee, we are unthinkingly causing moral injury. In modern suburbia, where the level of envy over cars and the size of houses and clothes runs unnecessarily high at times, we aggravate this situation by blackening the name or activities of another. This is especially important

14   Matthew 7:11.

to avoid in front of the children, for while adults may think their idle chatter harmless, overhearing children can quickly categorize and the harm may get passed on in overly absolute or exaggerated terms. Thus, Mr. Jones who acted a little foolishly after one too many Budweisers at the 4th of July picnic is known thereafter as a drunk, with probably a few other negative embellishments thrown in. Before long, the practice of detraction is carried over by children to their friends and classmates. This vice is well worth avoiding. Aren't the best people we know those who, in the colloquial, "have never had an unkind word about anyone"?

Finally, direct insults, while perhaps more honest than clandestine derision, are no more justifiable. In modern times, there has been an effort to use the law to proscribe so-called "hate speech," that is, insulting remarks directed at another because of race, ethnicity, gender, or religion. The law has had a very difficult time dealing with this, in part, because our constitutional system accords a wide berth for expressive freedom—at least against government censorship. Again, this illustrates how the law cannot do the work of morality. The virtue of justice imposes self-censorship of hateful remarks because they inflict unnecessary pain upon those to whom they are directed. Were this morality better affirmed, there would be no need to get bollixed up over whether the insult has some political point or redeeming social value. A moral commitment to justice avoids insult and averts the legal anxiety that results when government tries to regulate on the basis of content.

Any injury to reputation must be rectified as much as possible. It is a common complaint of those in public life, who bear much false criticism in banner headline, that the correction or response is seldom so prominently featured. Newspaper practice is thus not the moral ideal. If we cause hurt within our families, or outside, by injustice to reputation, we are called upon literally to take back our ugly words, and where our words have caused economic harm, pay compensation. Impossible? Perhaps. Certainly awkward. So awkward, in fact, that even the thought of having to make sufficient amends ought to chasten our behavior.

Family Checklist—Justice

1. *Respect God as the source of all existence.* Families manifest justice toward God in regular prayer, church attendance, maintaining a

family-oriented Sabbath, and by keeping faith with God at those times when human reality makes little sense.

2. *Justice depends upon a proper understanding of obligation.* Obligations flow from God through our defined human nature or as a result of promise or law. Families need to work in community to ensure that law does not contradict the natural obligations that arise especially from marriage and between parent and child.

3. *Family members have duties to community; the community has reciprocal duties to family members.* Among the most prominent of family duties owed to the community are to treat others with respect, to learn a trade or pursue knowledge, and to avoid causing harm. In return, the community owes individuals the preservation of the peace and the evenhanded distribution of *public* resources and burdens.

4. *Within families, understand how obligations of justice arise both by promise and as a matter of reciprocal love.* Young children owe their parents respect, obedience, and reasonable efforts toward the development of talent at home and in school. Older children have a filial obligation to care for elderly or disabled parents. The most important duty of parents is to see to their children's proper physical, intellectual, and spiritual education.

5. *Respect bodily integrity.* As a matter of justice, we must understand, and help our children understand from the earliest moment, that we do not own ourselves. Life is a gift not to be forfeited at the direction of personal will.

6. *Respect private property.* Private property is an important second principle closely related to bodily integrity, personal development, and community order. In this way, private property underlies the religious and other personal freedoms exercised by the family. Parents can manifest this respect in their own lives and inspire it in the actions of their children by treating the property of others with care, returning it promptly and in good condition, and accepting the privacy and decisions of owners.

7. *Speak well of others.* If criticism is made, it ought to be out of genuine interest in the improvement of the person criticized. Families must avoid talking ill of others,whether behind their backs or in an insulting and provoking manner in their presence. The control of hateful speech is more responsibly and justly accomplished through self-control taught within the family than censorship imposed by law on the nation at large.

8. *Be generous out of charity independent of legal obligation.* It is

important for families to avoid confusing charity with justice. Justice is that owed to another. Charity is that which is given freely out of love or generosity. Confusing these two concepts gives rise to specious claims of "rights" and involves the law in matters that should be handled by families.

9. *Act Truthfully and Authentically.* Honesty is a necessary support to the faithful performance of obligation and,thus, the fulfillment of justice. Families should encourage children to speak and act simply and openly. In our own dealings, we need to avoid sharp practice or overreaching.

10. *Where harm occurs, make restitution.* Harm can result out of willfulness or inadvertence. In either case, we have an obligation in justice to rectify the harm as completely as possible through personal service or the payment of compensation.

A Final Word about the Teaching of Virtue

Obviously, the morality encompassed in the virtue of justice, like that of prudence, temperance, and courage, is an aspiration. We will not always be paragons of virtue. But the message of the past two chapters is that our family pursuit of virtue will be advanced if we define our terms and then act in light of them as best we can. Leaving virtue undefined or encapsulated in vague formulations like "traditional values" invites neither an examination of family life or its improvement. Intellectuals fond of living in a world without moral absolutes may decry this effort as indoctrination. But as one author responded:

> The idea that we are indoctrinating children by encouraging them to be brave when they fall down or not to bear false witness or to bully or extort from their peers, would after all make sense only if there was some other alternative pattern of conduct in to which children might be reasonably initiated in the name of moral education. The only genuine positive alternative to encouraging children to be brave, self-controlled, honest, compassionate and so forth, however, is to instruct them in cowardice, self-indulgence, dishonesty and cruelty; but anyone who seriously held that these dispositions constitute a viable alternative moral code would, to say the very least, know the meaning of neither morality nor education.[15]

---

15   David Carr, *Educating the Virtues* (New York: Routledge, 1991), p.

Nor is it a meaningful alternative to teach our children nothing at all about virtue until they are old enough to think for themselves. Why? Because without the ability to act in a moral or virtuous manner, our children will be, quite literally, unable to think—ever.

243.

Chapter 9
Is the Family Up to the Task?

ALL ALONG, THE OBJECTIVE OF THIS BOOK has been to negotiate a successful conclusion or cease-fire to the culture war. The American family and its ability to revive cultural and personal virtue is critical to the effort. Is it up to the task?

Yes.

But before detailing some final practical steps that can terminate our present cultural hostility, let us briefly explore what it is we expect families to do and some reasons why these functions are not currently being performed as fully or as well as we like.

Family Expectations

Families are the central element in the personal lives of most Americans. Quite literally, the family structure introduces us to one another. As one author put it well: "[t]raditional society is composed of only two kinds of people—relatives and strangers. The social world centers around kinship identities, and relatives are those with whom you work, worship, ally, sleep, play, and die. Kinsmen bear you, nurse you in illness, initiate you into adulthood, protect you from injustice, and bury you into the order of the ancestors."[1] Looking at that list, it is quickly evident that every critical activity in life is performed with, through, or for the family.

A specific understanding of what families do, or are expected to do, can be categorized in two ways—from within the family or from the standpoint of society at large. Inside the family, research indicates that we envision the family as a source of "love and emotional support, respect for others, and taking responsibility for actions."[2] Behind the description of love or caring is the idea of

---

1   David W. Murray, "Poor Suffering Bastards," *Policy Review* (Spring 1994), p. 74.

2   Mark Mellman, Edward Lazarus, and Allan Rivlin, "Family Time,

constancy, family ritual. In other words, true emotional support is thought to be derived from being together for both important and unimportant times. The notion of "quality time" is thus seen as somewhat fraudulent, insofar as it suggests that family functions can be performed within a more limited time commitment.

Viewing the family as a basis for "respect for others" underscores the importance of the pursuit of personal virtue discussed in previous chapters. The terminology of prudence, fortitude, temperance, and justice may be unknown to the modern family, but there is a clear expectation that families build respect for people in authority, mutual respect between parent and child, and respect for others generally, in the sense of the Golden Rule or wanting to be dealt with fairly.

Finally, inside the family, we expect and want members of the family to do their jobs, to play their roles. Despite the increased number of mothers in the work force, common expectations still look to the father to work with regularity to provide the family income and to the mother to maintain the day-to-day functioning of the household. For the children, family expectations include punctual attendance and reasonable effort at school and a willingness to be helpful to parents and siblings without constant reminder or grousing.

Family functions may also be assessed from the outside; that is, from a societal, or cultural, perspective. These functions are often described as follows:

* *Having children*. Children do so much for us personally. They extend our earthly lives into a future that is not our own, and in the present, inspire gentleness and, most importantly, teach us to look beyond self. But the having of children has cultural or societal implications as well. These sociological or demographic or economic considerations sound, and in some ways, are more distant or remote than the personal emotions nurtured between a husband and wife by a child, but in their own way, they are significant.

Perhaps, the best way to understand what the having of children means to society at large is to examine the converse: that is, the consequences throughout the social system of having smaller families. Fewer children means fewer students. Fewer students means

---

Family Values," in *Rebuilding the Nest*, David Blankenhorn, Steven Bayne, Jean Bethke Elshtain, eds. (Milwaukee, Wis.: Family Service America, 1990), p. 73.

fewer schools and less investment in education and intellectual pursuits generally, from teaching to research and publication. Fewer children means fewer family units and less need for housing (fewer jobs for architects, builders, craftsmen, professionals, manufacturers of consumer goods and appliances and the blue-collar factory workers they would have otherwise employed). The corresponding decline in demand for existing housing means less "invested" equity or security and greater economic uncertainty with regard to retirement and health care for the previous generation. Overall, fewer children means less growth in gross domestic product and greater insecurity for everything and everybody dependent on that growth—publicly, for purposes of tax revenue to support ever-expanding programs like Medicare and Social Security or, privately, to create occupational opportunity.

* *Education for personal virtue.* Society expects families to form the moral character of their children; in the terms of this book, to instruct in prudence, fortitude, temperance, and justice as described earlier. The consequence of failing in these tasks is reflected in the increase in violent crime, and the decline in educational achievement and general levels of civility. One family researcher describes what is being lost as the family's unique capability "of keeping alive that combination of obligation and duty, freedom and dissent, that is the heart of democratic life."[3]

* *Education for personal happiness.* Society counts on families to produce a level of personal contentment necessary for social order. Happiness is something of an art. It requires a willingness to live in the present rather than to worry over the past or the future. Families are the best source of this perspective because both spouses and children emphasize the element of *now* to a larger degree than does business, government, and investment activity. These non-family activities, by their nature, are more often aimed at analyzing what happened or what is likely to happen. Happiness is also more apt to be derived from close relationships and leisure time, which again is more commonly associated with family, than not.

* *Sexual responsibility.* This is an aspect of personal virtue, but given the extraordinary levels of illegitimacy which Charles Mur-

---

3   Jean Bethke Elshtain, "The Family and Civic Life," in *Rebuilding, supra*, p. 128.

ray[4] describes as overshadowing every other social problem, it deserves separate listing.

* *Mediators between the state and the individual; between the economy and the individual.* A free-market, democratic society, in particular, needs the family to serve as an insulator from the intrusion of government and public demand as well as the similar attention commanded by the economic reality of having to make a living.

Family Realities

If these are the internal or personal and external or social expectations for the American family, are they being fulfilled, and if not, why not?

First, families aren't being established. It is presently estimated that between 20 and 25 percent of today's young women will remain childless all their lives and close to half will be childless or have one child.[5] The level of fertility generally is below that necessary for the mere replacement of the present population.

Second, if divorce is a measure, families are not happy. Levels of divorce have quadrupled over the past thirty years. "The probability that a marriage contracted today will end in divorce ranges from 44 to 66 percent, depending upon the method of calculation."[6]

Third, the family has not been successful, or has abandoned, its role in teaching sexual responsibility. Close to a third of all births are out of wedlock.[7] Surveys report high levels of sexual activity in children under the age of 18.

Fourth, time is being spent elsewhere. Families are not insulating from outside pressures because Mom and Dad are themselves outside exacerbating those pressures. Since 1965, families are

4   Charles Murray, "The Coming White Underclass," *Wall Street Journal* (October 29, 1993), p. A14.

5   David E. Bloom and James Trussell, "What Are the Determinants of Delayed Childbearing and Permanent Childlessness in the United States?" *Demography*, 21 (1984), pp. 591–611; Charles F. Westoff, "Perspective on Nuptiality and Fertility," *Population and Development Review* (Supp. No. 12 1986), pp. 155–70.

6   David Popenoe, "Family Decline in America," in *Rebuilding, supra*, p. 41.

7   U.S. Department of Health and Human Serivces, *Vital Statistics of the United States* (Washington, D.C.: Government Printing Office, 1993).

spending 40 percent less time together.[8] While in 1960, fewer than 20 percent of women with children under six were in the market-place, today the figure may be as high as 60 percent[9]

These are research statistics. They can vary; they can be manipulated; and they seldom tell the whole story. But the outline that emerges is worrisome. Given the importance, indeed the centrality, of the family to virtue and cultural peace, what ideas or factors lie behind these disturbing numbers?

☐ A shift from a focus on the family to a focus on what's in it for me. The "me" in this equation has been largely, though not exclusively, women seeking greater non-family or economic fulfillment, and employers, who because of labor shortages (triggered not unrelatedly by the smaller population base) need women employees in ever greater numbers.

☐ An inability and unwillingness on the part of *both* fathers *and* mothers to admit that family and work desires are in as great a conflict as they are. In an elevator, you cannot both go up and down at the same time. In life, you cannot both devote more time to work and to the family. Much that passes for pro-family public policy is actually pro-work public policy that makes it easier to accept the abandonment of traditional family responsibility. A good example is expanded public or private child care subsidies.

☐ As mothers have gone to work, fathers have disappeared. The rates of illegitimacy indicate that fathers are all too easily denying paternity, but even in the intact family, some fathers have forfeited their "provider" role as some mothers have distanced themselves from homemaking responsibility.[10]

☐ With work favored over family by both parents, family life is hectic and disoriented—often seeming out of control by any member of the family. The need to arrange child care itself, and the transportation involved, food shopping,

---

8   William R. Mattox, "The Family Time Famine," *Family Policy*, 3 (1990), p. 2.

9   Bureau of Labor Statistics, U.S. Department of Labor, *Employment in Perspective: Women in the Labor Force*, Fourth Quarter Report (Washington D.C., Government Printing Office, 1987): 749; see also, Popenoe, *supra*, p. 41.

10   See generally, Barbara Ehrenreich, *The Hearts of Men: American Dreams and the Flight From Commitment* (New York: Anchor).

house cleaning, school commitments, clothes washing, car maintenance, and many other basic activities pull families in multiple and opposing directions. One researcher reported a wry comment by a foreign colleague to the effect that "It seems to me in your country, most children are being brought up in moving vehicles."[11]

☐ Grandparents are missing. Some, including grandma, are still in the workforce, and many are in far away places for purposes of leisure and retirement.[12]

Family Resuscitated

In order to resuscitate the family, realities have to better match expectations. It might be tempting to say simply: "reverse course, full speed behind," but this is neither likely nor entirely desirable. The most prominent societal change affecting existing families is the attraction of women away from the full-time responsibilities of motherhood and homemakers and into the job market. This change has been salutary in some respects. Before women demonstrated their intellectual worth in the competing economic sphere, the law was irrationally discriminatory. Throughout the 19th century, state property laws, for example, deliberately prevented married women from contracting or owning property. Until 1920, women were denied even the right to vote.

And it was not only the law that treated mothers as second class; it was husbands and, often, children as well. Without a way to tangibly demonstrate their "worth" in economic terms, mothers, and the vital cultural role they play, were taken for granted. Like a reliable, but not flashy, employee in a large shop, the work got done well but without the deserved recognition needed to sustain it.

Family Prescription

* Honor Motherhood.

This is genuinely counter-cultural. It is also indispensable. As some recent teaching of the Catholic Church urges "the work of

---

11   Urie Bronfenbrenner, "The Changing Family in a Changing World" (unpublished) but cited in *Rebuilding, supra,* p. 35.

12   Victor Fuchs, "Are Americans Underinvesting in Children?" in *Rebuilding, supra,* p. 66. See also the excellent appraisal of this phenomenon and its consequences in Arthur Kornhaber and Kenneth L. Woodward, *Grandparents/Grandchildren* (New York: Anchor, 1981).

women in the home [must] be recognized and respected by all in its irreplaceable value. . . . [S]ociety must be structured in such a way that wives and mothers are *not in practiced compelled* to work outside the home. . . . [T]he mentality which honors women more for their work outside the home than for their work within the family must be overcome."[13]

If this prescription is to be followed, a decent family wage must be paid by all employers. Thirty years ago, in order to retain valued employees, employers necessarily had to consider the "whole family" in a wage offer. This may not have always been done overtly, but it was the inevitable consequence of the family relying upon principally one income. With both fathers and mothers in the marketplace, employers have had an easier time of it; wages can now be calculated and justified in relation to the needs of one person, married or single. More highly compensated employees may circumvent this somewhat with non-cash benefits, but even here, entirely proper notions of individual equality are used inappropriately and unthinkingly by employers to justify ignoring family circumstance. This is wrongheaded. The equal-pay act prohibits distinctions based on gender; it does not forbid asking whether an individual employee—whether man or woman—has the primary income responsibility for the family, and making wage offers accordingly. If the interpretation of the law does preclude this, it needs amendment. If families matter, they have to matter in rhetoric, law, and on the balance sheet.

Many employers recognize the ill-consequence of the disintegration of the family to their own bottom line. Unfortunately, this recognition also accepts as a uniform premise that what advances work, and especially what advances the work of both spouses, advances the family. Thus, most pro-family employer initiatives treat the family as an extraordinary or exceptional factor to be squeezed into the normal work day. The notion of a family-friendly workplace means simply that mothers and fathers can work with fewer interruptions from the family. Thus, the typical package of "forward-thinking" benefits includes full-day child care, flexible hours, job sharing, and the removal of stigma for time-off for a few family emergencies.

But this mentality, as understandable as it is coming from the

---

13   "The Role of the Christian Family in the Modern World," *Familiaris Consortio* (Boston: St. Paul Books and Media, 1981), pp. 40–41.

marketplace, has matters exactly backwards from the standpoint of the revival of the family and its contribution to cultural peace. It is not the family that is the interruption; it is work. Work is a positive and noble good, but from the vantage-point of advancing the strongest possible family foundation with a full-time parent at home, these corporate initiatives miss the mark. As one research study concluded after examining these programs:

> [W]e shouldn't fool ourselves that the interests of the working parent—or the interests of the corporation—are identical to those of the child. . . . [C]ompanies are mostly interested in easing the lives of working parents so that these employees can devote more "quality time" to the firm.[14]

The push toward work and away from family is echoed, and worsened, in government tax policy. Every American feels over-taxed, but families really are. For most of the period since 1960, the average tax rate as a percentage of income did *not* increase for single Americans or those who were married without children, but for the American family with four children, average tax rates increased 233 percent.[15] How did this inequity get enacted into law? Largely, by clever omission. Each time the tax rates were increased, the personal exemption, with rare exception, stayed the same. As a consequence, tax increases have been inequitably loaded onto families, thereby creating economic pressure for both spouses to be in the workforce. Unfortunately, only a handful of pro-family Congressmen and Senators can be heard calling for personal exemptions for children to be increased.

Employer and government policy aside, mothers must not fail to honor themselves. That's right, mothers need to stop apologizing in public and private conversation for being mothers. When meeting someone new, the answer isn't, "I'm just a housewife" or "I don't work." Goodness knows, every mother I have ever met is working constantly. A friend of ours who is the mother of seven accomplished children is married to a well-respected criminal-law professor. When they lived in Washington D.C., they would fre-

---

14   Sylvia Ann Hewlett, "Good News? The Private Sector and Win-Win Scenarios," in *Rebuilding, supra,* p. 215.

15   *Mandate for Leadership III Policy Strategies for the 1990s,* Charles L. Heatherly and Burton Yale Pines, eds. (Washington, D.C.: Heritage Foundation, 1989), p. 452.

quently be invited to social receptions. When guests at these receptions asked what she did, she noticed that when she responded "mother," people would turn away. To alleviate this, she began cleverly responding "early childhood education," which would keep the conversation going apace. Our friend was clever and very accommodating—too accommodating to a culture that may not actually disrespect motherhood but is far too willing to ignore its worth. Mothers, please don't contribute to this. Fly your standard proudly.

Family Prescription

* Husbands, Honor Your Wives

This is somewhat different from honoring motherhood, but it is clearly related. Honoring motherhood, as noted above, is designed to facilitate the natural relationship between mother and child by making it more feasible, in terms of wages and the like, for a mother to be at home with her children. By comparison, this prescription is aimed at reminding husbands that they have a special debt to their wives for the personal sacrifice that a wife and mother makes in devoting her intellectual talents and efforts to the maintenance of the family home and the raising of children, rather than external, marketplace pursuits that pay far better and lead to public recognition.

How can husbands tangibly give wives this honor? First, husbands ought never assume the attitude that what they are doing during most of the day is more important than what is going on at home. Truth be told, whatever husbands do working outside the home is but a means to the end that mothering is in the thick of, namely, the maintenance of a solid and stable family life. No modern husband expecting to remain physically intact would come right out and assert the superiority of his job, but it may unfortunately be implicit in a condescending tone or questions at the end of the day that take the form of an auditor of accounts: "And what went on around here today?" Husbands need to be interested in their wives' routine out of love and respect for the challenges of being a mother and a desire to be helpful, not out of envy or an immature comparison of who is "doing more" each day in a scorekeeping sense.

Second, husbands must be more sensitive to expanding mothers' careers and intellectual possibilities over time. As a family moves beyond the care of young children, husbands and wives ought to recalibrate the allocation of work/family responsibilities so that both spouses can fairly, and at different times during the marriage, experience the challenge of both career and family obligation. This may mean that a husband forgoes a promotion or career opportunity in order that a wife may assume one. Alternatively, Dad may commit to being at home earlier or in the evenings to permit mom to re-enroll in the university or vocational training.

Family Prescription

* Elevate the family over "money and power" systems.

Work and family; government and family are best seen as competitors. Work demands our dedication, our intellect, and the best hours in our day. If both mother and father are working, family gets the leftovers. Politics and government too compete with the family. It was the family that once provided for its elderly members. It was the family that once directed and financed a child's education. It was the family that provided moral instruction over questions such as sexual abstinence. Today, these functions for most Americans have been given over to politics and the government: Social Security and Medicare for the elderly, the public-school system, school-based sex education and clinics and federal laws such as the Adolescent Family Life Act. For the poor, the government *is* the family; it is all of the above and food and shelter as well. The proposed health-care reforms merely continue this preference for government over family.

Noted writer Robert Bellah describes this as a conflict between the "lifeworld" (that is, the family where we learn the right way to act) and money and power "systems." Bellah observes:

> Of course, we need a good government and a good economy. It is not a question of abolishing them, but of putting the proper limits on them. . . .
>
> The job culture is indeed crowding out the family culture, given the economic pressures of our era. The invasion of the "lifeworld" by the market economy is complex and multilayered. Many women have had to go to work just to keep things level, given a variety of economic pressures. But the amount of time people work is due to more than necessity. . . .
>
> . . . [T]he quality of much day care is doubtful and even the

best day care cannot make up for lack of parental attention. If both parents are working, and perhaps working for excessive hours, not to meet the basic necessities of life but to pay for what they think is a preferred style of life because of the pressures of consumerism, family life can suffer as a consequence.[16]

"He who pays the piper, calls the tune." It is no more complicated than that. If we really want families to have greater authority, *we* must personally—in our attitude toward work and for what we are working—and as a national community in our understanding of the role of government, put families first.

Family Prescription

* Spend the time

Families need time more than anything else. Parental time. We know we are shortchanging our families. In recent research, close to 90 percent of those surveyed recognized that families are spending less time together than thirty years ago.[17] The inadequacy of family time is especially acute in two-income, divorced, and single-parent families. Levels of family happiness and satisfaction are strongly correlated with adequate time with the family—defined in terms of survey response as better than 50 percent of waking time.

Family Prescription

* Families need a sense of place; community

Too many families are rootless. We move from city to city at the call of employers. We pursue advanced educations as a way out of home and community, or at least without giving thought to the leaving. Community has become a place to be until graduation or marriage or the next job or retirement. Options are kept open and fluid. And as a consequence, whatever moral instruction occurs within the family cannot be backed up by the sanction of being

---

16   Robert N. Bellah, "The Invasion of the Money World," in *Rebuilding, supra*, p. 227.

17   Mellman, et al., in *Rebuilding, supra*, p. 88,

known and measured by neighbors. If we are just passing through, what do we care what they think? Without community attachment and sanction, the pursuit of cultural virtue is limited to self-interest, personal calculation, or charity. We get involved as it suits us. Virtue requires more than just self-satisfaction or personal fulfillment; it *obligates* to family and community. It obligates to families *in* community.

Family Prescription

* Set Family Policy In Relation to the Desired Norm

What is the desired norm? Ask a child. Would she rather have both a father and a mother or just a mother? Would the child like to see her parents more or less frequently during the day? Where would the child prefer to be—at home or in a day-care institution? When the child is ill, would she rather be in the care of a paid employee-stranger or Mom or Dad?

We know the answers to these questions. We know the norm.

And, if as we know, the two-parent, one-income family within a marriage relationship that takes lifetime commitment seriously is the desired norm, then any public policy or private preachment must clearly recognize this as the preferred form of family life. Along similar lines we would do well not to understate the continued existence of the desired family norm. Congresswoman Patricia Schroeder is fond of saying that to set family policy in light of the "needs of the traditional family is like saying the highway program must recognize people who don't drive."[18] That glib statement, however often repeated, is a caricature of the truth, as David Blankenhorn has shown with government statistics that find the desired norm *even today* to be the "nation's largest single category of families with preschool children."[19]

Compassion, as informed by the theological virtue of charity, demands that we extend our hand to those whose circumstances do not put them within the desired norm; for example, those who

---

18   Patricia Schroeder (with Andrea Camp and Robyn Lipner), *Champion of the Great American Family* (New York: Random House, 1989), p. 84.

19   David Blankenhorn, "American Family Dilemmas," in *Rebuilding, supra* p. 13, showing that the norm comprised over a third of all families.

are suffering the malady of divorce or who have lost their spouse to an early death. Reason and cultural stability, however, require that we not confuse compassion and affirmation.

Advancing the desired family norm may mean everything from cajoling the media to more consistently and responsibly portray the family in this way in television and movie production, to making divorce less accessible or automatic (a direct reversal of the 1960–90 trend toward "no-fault" divorce), to assisting in the development of more meaningful and church-based marriage and family preparation and dispute resolution assistance. Every church congregation needs a well-motivated team of "marriage paramedics."

Family Prescription

    * Understand what it means to be a family

The prevalent culture is based on radical individualism. We go our separate ways as spouses. We leave the children to do the same. Out of this extreme autonomy, we have come to doubt both moral truth and the scientific facts of our own natures. We brandish rights and are unaware of duty. In doing so, we have been provoked to the brink of cultural war, and perhaps beyond. This is *learned* behavior. "Before the shooting begins," to borrow the phraseology of the chronicler of culture war, it must be *unlearned*.

It can be *unlearned*. It is not too late. We must put aside the distractions of television, the confusion of morality with law and the distortions of left-right politics, and set about our family's business in earnest. What is this business? What are families about?

Just this:

- ☐ conquering the harshness and isolation of traveling through life alone with a marriage relationship built on support and lifetime commitment, not domination and individual want;

- ☐ having children out of a desire to be loving cooperators in God's gift of life, not because it is the thing to do or because of what children are thought to do for us;

- ☐ being cultural educators of the first-rank; nurturing the physical, intellectual, moral, and spiritual formation of children; unashamedly and clearly transferring to them the mega-virtues of belief in God and a knowable truth and the personal, cardinal virtues of prudence, fortitude, temperance, and justice;

☐ understanding that schools are extensions of responsible parenting, not replacements for it;

☐ welcoming and encouraging the continued presence of our own parents in the lives of our children, not merely as babysitters, but as family elders connecting the past with the present and thus valued for their family and cultural wisdom;

☐ making our family a part of a network of families united by faith and active in church, and open to its moral instruction. Churches are strong allies of families in the pursuit of virtue because by nature they too obligate. What's more, they provide a necessary insulation from the corrosive skepticism of modern culture.

☐ making our family a part of a network of families united by place, a local community, not just as a stop along the career or educational highway.

Within the family, cultural peace is at hand. We must merely reach for it.

Chapter 10
Concluding Perspectives on the American Family

DURING THE WRITING OF THIS BOOK, I had occasion to reflect on a great many matters confronting the traditional American family. Most of these thoughts are set out formally in the previous chapters. Some ideas, however, were free-standing, as it were, and over time, I developed them into short commentaries. Often, I tested these opinions out in the editorial pages of the *Chicago Tribune, Wall Street Journal,* or other leading newspapers, and many more were part of a popular radio series entitled "The American Family Perspective."[1] I hope you enjoy or benefit from them too.

Whatever Happened to Good Family Movies?

Ever wonder why old movies are generally better for families than today's features?

There is a great deal of talk right now about excessive violence and sex on television and in the movie theater. Even the Attorney General of the United States, Janet Reno, has threatened to "look into matters," if Hollywood doesn't clean up its act.

The government has a problem disciplining these things, however. For good reason, the First Amendment protects us from government censorship.

But being free of government censorship doesn't mean that movie producers should be free of their own. It used to be that those who made movies and those who wrote scripts understood that they had an obligation to be good citizens, to preserve and portray the best in our culture and to encourage us all to aim high.

From the 1930s through the 1950s, producers abided by the

---

1   I am most grateful to WFRN-FM of Elkhart, Indiana, for generously assisting me with the radio production of the series.

self-imposed Motion Picture Production Code. Among its many provisions, the code cautioned that films must not make criminals seem heroic and justified, impure love must never be presented as attractive, the use of firearms should be restricted to "essentials," and the courts of the land should not be presented as unjust.

Today, of course, movies and television pursue just the opposite: criminals are superheroes; love is almost always *divorced* from marriage, commitment, and family; and firearms are everywhere—in schools, offices, and even churches.

When the code was followed, however, it was a different, and better, story. Jimmy Stewart took Mr. Smith to Washington and in the process taught every one of us about the importance of integrity in government. Gary Cooper wrestled with his Biblical faith and the demands of a world war in *Sergeant York*. On television, Perry Mason fought for justice, Ben Casey sought to heal the sick, and Lucy made us laugh at ourselves. And yes, even Ozzie and Harriet brought more simple honesty to the portrayal of everyday life within the family than, say, Roseanne.

Oh, maybe sometimes the shows were heavy on the syrup, but if and when they were, it was always in pursuit of a noble virtue: love, loyalty, courage, hard work, marital fidelity. Not only is this not the theme of the modern television and film industry, it often seems as if they have these virtues targeted for extinction or ridicule.

We need the film and television business to shape up. They need to once again understand the simple truth written in the preamble of their own code from the 1930s, that entertainment has a moral importance. It enters intimately into the lives of men and women; it affects them closely; it occupies their minds and affections during leisure hours; and ultimately touches the whole of their lives.

Yes, it sure does. And what is touching the whole of our lives today is a form of electronic leprosy that invades the minds of the young and old alike with lurid sex and violence and disrespect for everything that in our saner moments we would cherish and respect.

Craftsmen of every type know that men and women are judged by the quality of their work. By this measure, much of Hollywood today merits no stars and two thumbs down.

Welfare Reform, The Family and Charity

Welfare Reform.

The very words are almost enough to make the eyes glaze over.

Yet, the welfare mess does need attention, and we would do well to listen to people like Michael Bauman, director of Christian studies at Hillsdale College in Michigan. In a recent essay, Dr. Bauman reminds us that St. Paul separates the deserving from the undeserving poor. "If a man will not work, St. Paul writes, he shall not eat."[2]

Simple recognition of this principle of charity, in itself, would end welfare as we know it—where it is possible to obtain more tax-free funds for doing nothing than it is to earn on some jobs after taxes. In a truly reformed welfare system, only diligent workers and the genuinely unable would get help; everyone else would get our best wishes and the moral exhortation to get busy.

True charity also would avoid funneling assistance through the government. First, the government ends up spending more on welfare administrators than the deserving poor. The figures are in the trillions'—enough that had the money been given directly, there wouldn't be a man, woman, or child beneath the poverty line.

Second, working through the government deadens the charitable spirit. When we are content to let bureaucrats handle the poverty unpleasantness, we deal with people in a nameless, faceless way —not as co-members of church and community.

Third, the government almost always ends up subsidizing immorality. Just as too much auto insurance can aggravate the cost of accidents—why not, says the repair shop, have the whole fender replaced rather than repaired since insurance is paying—so too welfare increases the likelihood of illegitimate children and absentee fathers.

Avoiding the government, by the way, doesn't mean sloughing off responsibility for the poor on business or property owners either. To be sure, the virtue of justice requires a fair wage and a fair price. But raising minimum wages to unrealistic levels or imposing rent controls often perversely injures, rather than helps, the poor.

If wages are artificially high, those with the least skills are simply not hired, or the products made with high wages are too overpriced to be purchased. As Bauman puts it, if the government mandated a minimum price of $25,000 for American cars to help the ailing auto workers in Detroit, the only beneficiaries would be the Japanese.

---

2   2 Thess. 3:10.

So what is to be done? One attractive idea is to reunite welfare contributor and recipient. Eliminate the middle man, be it government or the coercive mandates on business and property owners. Instead, let taxpayers subtract from their tax bill—dollar for dollar—every amount given to a bonafide charity, church, relief organization, homeless shelter, or training center.

Will this end poverty? No. Sadly, it is part of the human condition. But families can help each other far more directly and far more effectively, then when the government pretends to play "good samaritan."

Dead Serious

Is there a constitutional right to commit suicide?

Families confronting unprecedented levels of teenage suicide need a straight answer. The answer is "No."

Washington state has a statute that makes promoting a suicide of another a felony. When this statute was challenged as a "civil rights" violation last year, Federal District Judge Barbara Rothstein startled a culture already reeling from extraordinary rates of family breakdown, abortion, and illegitimacy, with the proposition that the right to choose death is simply another aspect of personal choice.

Ostensibly, the district judge tried to limit her freakish legal creation of an unfettered suicide right to the terminally ill, but in this, there proved no meaningful stopping point. Thankfully, she has now been forcefully reversed on appeal. As the federal appellate court found, once the right to take one's life is claimed as a matter of personal liberty, there is no way of keeping it from "the depressed twenty-one year old, the romantically-devastated twenty-eight year old, or the alcoholic forty-year old."

Even if one assumed a suicide right could be confined to the "terminally ill," who falls within this category? A terminal illness can vary from days or weeks to years with AIDS and some forms of cancer. Other illnesses related to heart disease are curable with a transplant; is this within the category of terminal illness? In truth, "life itself is a terminal condition . . . ."

The now-rejected suicide right had no support in the 205 years of our constitutional existence. It was a prime example of judicial law making "unknown to the past and antithetical to the defense of human life," that the appellate court reasoned was "a chief responsibility of our constitutional government." After all, the Declaration of Independence intended to be implemented by the Constitution declares life an "unalienable right." And "unalienability" precisely means that it is incapable of being forfeited or transferred by anyone.

Beyond its distortion of the Constitution, and disregard of the "self-evident" truths in our declaration of national purpose, the invented suicide right had the capacity of turning physicians as healers into physicians as killers. Only when doctors are committed to curing illness and disease are they committed to medical progress. When doctors facilitate suicide, they facilitate medical failure. As far as medical treatment is concerned, it is literally a "dead-end."

So too, the existence of the putative suicide right put enormous psychological pressure on the elderly and the disabled. We have all been taught to "do what the doctor orders," and as a New York commission found, "[o]nce the physician suggests suicide or euthanasia, some patients will feel that they have few, if any alternatives, but to accept the recommendation."

This is especially true of the poor. Pain can be a strong encouragement for suicide, and the poor have far less means of alleviating pain. In these days of reduced public expenditure, there is but a short distance between the false proclamation of a personal suicide right and the generalized calculation that this might well reduce the overall cost of public assistance.

The law has always recognized a "right to be let alone" in the sense of allowing each of us to avoid the infliction of medical procedures against our will. Faith traditions differ as to when medical assistance can be morally declined, with many drawing the line at extraordinary care of no benefit to the patient. But neither the law nor morality has ever likened the informed withdrawal or withholding of useless or extraordinary medical treatment with a "right to let others [especially another licensed by the state] to mutilate or kill you."

The district judge had premised her now-overthrown personal-suicide right on the controversial abortion right. The appellate court thought this "an enormous leap, doing violence to context and ignoring the difference between the regulation of reproduction and the promotion of killing a patient at his or her request." In truth, for many Americans who have been chary of the abortion business all along, the acceptance of choice of death at life's beginning was certain to lead to the endorsement of similar choice near life's end. Once freedom is untethered from responsibility, it is license, even a license to kill.

The doctors who sought the right to take the lives of their patients no doubt were motivated by a desire to end horrendous suffering. In this, they acted out of compassion. But compassion, like freedom without responsibility, is not the totality of life. Compassion can indeed lead to tragedy when it is unguided by the restraining virtues of justice and prudence and courage.

Reuniting Home and Work

There is an inevitable tension in most families between the demands of work and home. Where both parents work outside the home, this pressure is especially evident—with rushed breakfasts; hurried trips to schools or day care; the stress of doctor's visits when the inevitable flu arrives; dinner times that are delayed by overtime on the job or constantly interrupted by school-related sports activities that always seem to fall right at the dinner hour. A relaxed moment between parent and child occurs, if at all, with the wish of a good night. Unfortunately, in the morning, the marathon begins again.

This is not a healthy family environment, and, apparently, it wasn't always this way. According to Nancy Pearcy in an article for the Rockford Institute Center on the Family,[3] before the middle of the 19th century, the two fundamental tasks of making a living and raising children were often one.

Many mothers and fathers worked side-by-side on farms; others ran small household industries, from weaving to baking to carpentry. With the advent of the modern office and factory, however, several things happened. At first, Dad left home to seek outside work. This oriented Dad to the nonfamily, dog-eat-dog culture, and left Mom to be dependent, alone. While, at first mothers took up the burden of passing on traditional values at home to the children, soon Dad's work-orientation and individualism infected her too.

The modern result: Dad and Mom are both in the workplace. The tension between home and work has been resolved—in favor of work.

---

3   Nancy R. Pearcy, "Rediscovering Parenthood in the Information Age," *The Family in America*, 8, No. 3 (March 1994).

Is the modern result a good one in terms of life's primary goal: the leading of a good or virtuous life, informed by the word of God, ultimately, leading to salvation?

Hardly. The nightly newspapers tell the story—staggering rates of juvenile crime, illegitimacy, drug and alcohol abuse—in short, cultural disintegration led by family break-up.

Can we find our way back? Can we reunite home and work? While returning to the farm for most of us is impossible, it may not be unthinkable for some work to come home. New technology allows this so-called "telecommuting," and it involves using computers, fax machines, internet, and the like to do everything from stock market investing to inventory management to business and insurance reports to commercial artistry.

Is this a pipe dream? No, over 39 million Americans now work at home either full or part-time. And there are mutual benefits for work and family. Employers have found sharp increases in productivity and less employee turnover. There is also a marked reduction in pollution since there are fewer people on the road.

But most importantly, telecommuting has started to resurrect the pre-19th century ideal of Dad and Mom working side-by-side, often at different work tasks, but jointly and genuinely invested in the lives and moral growth of their children. Now that's real progress.

"Evangelizing Marriage"

Consider two facts:

Fact No. 1: The number of illegitimate births in the United States is skyrocketing. According to the *USA Today*, each year one in every sixteen teenage girls has a baby. In many states, the percentage of unwed births has nearly doubled over the past ten years from 15 percent to close to 30 percent. In some inner cities, the percentages are staggeringly higher.

Fact No. 2: The number of children being born to married couples is now below the so-called replacement level; that is, the number of children within marriages is below 2—something like 1.8 children per married woman.

In the first case, we get children who are unwanted, and destined for a life of poverty, crime, and illiteracy; in the second, children who are needed to maintain the community but aren't there.

We are told by more than a few political figures that the solution to the first problem—illegitimacy and teenage pregnancy—is the wider distribution of condoms and contraceptives and the greater availability of abortion. This is lunacy. Not only have such contraceptive measures proved ineffective, they are immoral.

The modern politician has no comment on the second fact—declining births within marriage. After all, they tell us, to suggest that wives have children and that husbands and wives together devote more of themselves to family than career is distinctly unmodern.

But here's news for our political friends, a society where the number of children born to the immature and irresponsible is rapidly increasing and the number of children born to the capable and committed is declining is a society that will soon fall of its own weight.

Illegitimacy and fewer children do, of course, have a common origin—namely, selfishness. In the one case, it is a selfish, unthinking desire for sexual gratification; in the other, it is the overriding desire for career advancement and personal fulfillment.

The solution lies not in condoms or school-based clinics on the one hand or in government exhortations about the necessity of a sufficiently large and well-motivated population, but in us.

That's right, if we want this done right—we are going to have to do it ourselves. Those of us who are married have a sacred duty to evangelize the very sanctity and nobility of marriage. When it is written in Hebrews that "Marriage is honorable in all," we are being instructed to treat married life as an honor, a noble calling—not a second thought. This means not being shy about instructing our teenagers in the importance and beauty of love and procreation within marriage. Giving them the courage and the well-thought-out responses to resist the sexually saturated television entertainment and peers they confront. It means guiding our college-aged children to put family, not career, first.

And above all, it means that we must do the same.

The Family Friendly Neighborhood

Is your neighborhood family-friendly?

Sure, you might say, we have many friendly families. But that's not the question, is your neighborhood—its physical lay-out, design, or restrictions—family-friendly?

This requires a little more thought. A quick look around may reveal nice lawns, comfortable looking houses, and if you're close to my home base in Indiana, a fair number of basketball hoops, but these things in themselves do not a family-friendly neighborhood make.

What does?

Here are a few things to ask yourself. If Grandma or Grandpa needed or wanted to be closer, would local regulation allow you to create a separate apartment for them in your home? Or if you live out where there is more space, could you locate a separate mobile or manufactured home for them in the yard?

When you need a loaf of bread or a gallon of milk, can you ask your nine or ten year old to walk over to a nearby store to get it, or must you hop in the car and drive to the superstore on the errand yourself?

So too, when you go off to church on Sunday, is it around the corner or miles away?

If computer technology and the like allow you to run your small business from your home, could you do it legally?

The most common answer to all of these and similar questions is no. And here's why:

The American planning or zoning model in city and suburb alike for the past forty years or so has been one of strict-use segregation. Houses for nuclear—not extended—families in one place, businesses in another, stores in a third, and churches still somewhere else. This creates a nice, neat, everything-in-its-place, appearance, but the design has real problems too.

For years, engineers have recognized that this type of land-use arrangement aggravates the problem of the automobile—most notably, air pollution. But mothers and fathers can verify that having to drive everywhere—school, store, church, library, park, office—is not healthy either.

And what's worse, this land-use arrangement, which we allow to exist in our local laws and even accept under so-called private restrictive covenants in the suburbs, creates sterile, isolated environments that breed juvenile boredom and separates, rather than unifies, families.

Even as 40 percent of working Americans will soon be faced with making some care arrangements for elderly grandparents, zoning laws keep Grandma and Grandpa—or even a newly married son or daughter struggling to get on his or her feet—from moving into an easily created separate apartment or house on your own property. The same laws keep convenient stores and small retail shops, even those with well-appointed signs and no heavy truck deliveries or parking problems, far away. Youngsters are thus deprived of the responsibility of doing family shopping or the opportunity of an after-school or summer part-time job. And many of us are forced to drive great distances for some work that could just as easily be done at or near home.

It doesn't have to be this way. Many European towns and cities, for example, have never accepted our monotonous zoning model. Closer to home, we could create or allow existing neighborhood associations to authorize all of these varied uses in our neighborhoods in a compatible, sensible way.

Maybe this spring as the home developers make their usual show of fancy new homes with sparkling oval windows and expensive chandeliers, we might ask them whether the zoning laws and restrictions in these new "estates" are family-friendly. If not, maybe it's time for our families to vote with their feet.

Private Property and the American Family

Sometimes we understate the value of "things." And here I really mean things—that is, private property.

To be sure, the Bible directs us not to be materialistic, not to be concerned with the things of this world. But we should not lose sight that property is also part of God's creation and that He enjoined us to assert dominion over it for good purposes.

One of the reasons our nation has flourished has been its bedrock respect for private property. James Madison went so far as to say that the essential purpose of the American Constitution was the protection of property. The Constitution itself reflects this in the Bill of Rights, when it provides that government may not "take" private property for public use without just compensation.

What does private property do for us? It permits us to express our talents and personalities; it permits us to exercise our liberties. The items we make and the homes we live in reveal much about who we are. When we teach children to respect another child's toys, we are teaching them to respect the other child.

Obviously, private property is also critical to the family. The possession of a safe, quiet home base allows for leisure and learning activities that are vital to the success of a family.

Finally, private property in the workplace provides incentives for us to share our talents and resources. The food grown in the field by the farmer and put upon the shelf by the grocer, the electronic gear made in the factory, the book written in the library are all examples of private property being used, and then created anew, to connect us with others, to help others through our personal efforts.

The importance of private property to a good life suggests why it is very troublesome when government undertakes activities that disregard this principle.

Consider two Supreme Court cases: one decided a few years back, and one more recently. Awhile ago, Jim and Marilyn Nollan wanted to expand their small house, which happened to be nicely located along the ocean. The Nollans were told that they could get a building permit for their new home only if they granted free access over part of their property to the general public. The Nollans properly objected, and the Court took their side.

So too, John and Florence Dolan came before the Court. The Dolans wanted a permit to expand their plumbing-supply store. The City of Tigard, Oregon, said yes, but only if John and Florence gave the city 10 percent of their land for a bicycle path. The Dolans refused, and again, the U.S. Supreme Court found the government to be overreaching.

The Nollans and Dolans won, but only after years of litigation leading to the highest court in the land. Property owners can seldom afford this; yet the problems these families confronted are not isolated ones. In some states, local governments have been demanding, for example, that the builders of new homes donate land for day-care centers, funds for multicultural activities, and a host of other things on municipal wish lists from expressways to fire engines.

In themselves, the items demanded are not evil. What is evil is singling out an individual property owner, who is at the mercy of government power, to provide them. These government demands are often the equivalent of extortion. In essence, the government says, if you wish to make a lawful use of your property and you want a permit for it, give us money or goods or give us part of your land. Not quite as stark as "Your money or you life," but not far different, either. Failure to ante up means no permit.

This disregard of private property burdens many families. Obviously, it directly affects property owners like Jim and Marilyn and John and Florence, but it also affects you and me. Fewer houses are built, fewer jobs created, and lives dependent upon the stability of property interests are disrupted.

And worst of all, a government founded to protect property (and the human persons and liberty that property represents) is in some cases destroying it.

Religious Freedom in Favor of the Traditional Family is Not Discrimination

Two brothers, Ron and Paul Desilets, own an apartment building in Turners Falls, Massachusetts. They are Catholic and they take their faith seriously.

Recently, Cynthia Tarail wanted to rent a unit in their apartment house. The Desilets refused. You see, Cynthia was not going to occupy it alone, or with her husband, but with her live-in boyfriend, Mark Lattanzi.

The Desilets didn't think that was right. Sexual relations outside of marriage is forbidden by the Catholic church, as it is by many religious denominations. What's more, said the Desilets, it violates state law—a law that today often is ignored, but nevertheless, expressly prohibits fornication.

The Desilets have assumed a highly principled and, as it turns out, costly moral position.

It seems that while the state attorney general in Massachusetts is quite willing to disregard the laws against illicit sex, he is very anxious to enforce another statute passed in this age of permissiveness that prohibits so-called "discrimination on the basis of marital status."

I said so-called "discrimination" because it is vitally important for those taking the mega-virtues seriously to object when the drawing of legitimate and morally important distinctions is pejoratively described as discrimination.

The Desilets aren't excluding on the basis of race or because their rental applicants are of one political party or another. No, the Desilets are simply, and straightforwardly, expressing and acting upon unquestioned religious instruction.

The true characterization of this story is not one of improper discrimination but of interference with religious freedom. Even if the state law ostensibly prohibits drawing the common-sense distinction between those men and women who formally commit their lives to each other in marriage and those who "unite temporarily" for purposes of sexual gratification, the First Amendment to the Constitution should guarantee the "free exercise of religion" upon which such distinction is also based.

As interpreted by the Supreme Court, however, the Constitution has not always taken the side of the traditional family and religious freedom. According to case decision, as long as laws do not single out religion for special hostility, a general law—like that in Massachusetts inviting the family-destroying practice of cohabitation—could be enforced.

In late 1993, Congress passed the Religious Freedom Restoration Act. In a nutshell, the act provides that when general laws impede or burden religious beliefs or practice, like that of the Desilets, the government must supply a very compelling justification or provide a religious exemption.

For lawyers, there is some constitutional doubt whether Congress can in essence "overrule" the Supreme Court's misinterpretation of the religious freedom provisions of our Constitution. But this much is clear, the drafters of the First Amendment made religious belief and practice America's first freedom, and that's what Congress' new legislation attempts to rescue from the Court's error.

The Massachusetts attorney general ultimately dropped the charges against the Desilets for reasons of "time and money," without conceding the validity of the brothers' faith-based argument. It will now be left to other landlords in other places to articulate as well as the Desilets that law is not morality, and on some unfortunate occasions, law is even in opposition to it.

The Family and The Corporation

We often hear these days that the 1980s was the "decade of greed." In actual fact, however, economists who aren't working one or the other side of the political street will tell you honestly that the 1980s was a time of economic growth and optimism in which over 20 million new jobs were created.

Today, things seem a bit less optimistic. At various times, this may be because of increasing interest rates, the uncertainty of government reform, or even foreign threat. In truth, the cause may lie deeper. It may have more to do with the fact that we've lost sight of how noble it is to run a business, to provide jobs for people, to seek to deliver quality goods and services.

That's right, we've been told so often about "corporate fat cats" and the like that we have forgotten that a business corporation is a vital social institution—perhaps, second in importance only to the family and its church.

One of the most interesting features of early America was its preoccupation with teamwork, with voluntary association. This is perhaps not wholly surprising as the only way wildernesses in new and unmapped territory would be cleared for farms and shops was with neighbor helping neighbor. In this atmosphere, the business corporation was a prime example of the "I will" or "can do" spirit. "The impossible takes a little longer" was the spirit of the day, says author Michael Novak.

And the corporation—running a business—has a sound moral footing as well. It is through this organization of individual talent that creative human work occurs. And in this work, not only is wealth created, but man's own nature is transformed. The virtues of diligence, industriousness, prudence, taking reasonable risks, reliability, and loyalty are sharpened and instilled.

Sometimes the press or various political figures refer to businessmen as "profit-mongers," but much religious teaching acknowledges profit as a proper goal—because the existence of a reasonable profit reveals that human needs are being met.

New businesses bring new jobs. And with new jobs comes hope and generosity. Without respect for those who risk their fortunes trying out a new product or trying to deliver an old one better, we degenerate into a society of envy. In this, the founders of America recognized that the quickest way to end democracy was to encourage the envy of one faction or another.

Unfortunately, envy seems to be a driving force in modern politics and life, though we sometimes insidiously hide envy under banners of "justice" or "equality." But envy is seldom conquered by categorical demand or government edict. Rather, envy is overcome by a genuine willingness to associate with others in a new venture that utilizes the skills of others and nourishes their hopes in a realistic way for a better life.

We owe a debt of gratitude to the men and women in our community who run the shops, who build the homes, who had the courage and initiative to run businesses that make all our lives better, and in the process, give free rein to God-given talents.

Decade of Greed—Baloney. Let us just pray that we can get past these years of envy.

A Family's Happiness Depends on You

What does it take for a family to be happy?

The answer: "You."

You have the capacity to make yourself happy and share it with your family, in God's wisdom.

God told Moses: "I am, Who am." Notice that this declaration is in the present tense. God isn't a person from the past or something that might or might not happen in the future—He is now, in the present, walking with you, counseling you and your family, if only you let Him.

But we don't listen to God's counsel if we are always fretting over that which is past or anxious about something that is going to happen tomorrow. Worse, we don't see God now, in the little children who depend on us, in our spouses, or in our neighbors because we are too distracted with a past or a future that, in faith, we ought to submit to God's will and assessment.

God said: "I am, Who Am." He is with us now; if we are prepared to join Him.

What does this mean practically?

First, it means see those who are around you now.

Appreciate your spouse. Compliment him or her on a dinner made or a home-improvement chore accomplished.

Learn about your children. Talk with them. So often, children chatter, but parents do not fully listen. Distracted by adult things—fixing dinner or getting to work or the NBA final on TV—parents sometimes half listen. How very much is missed in the half that is not heard! The new friend at school, difficulty or achievement in a particular class, a question about how to handle a problem.

Second, it means taking a close look at what you are doing now. Management experts recommend that people make lists before they leave the office at night. What's the purpose of the list? To take stock of the present situation. To see what is being done now. Make a list on paper or in your mind of what are you doing in your family life too. If every day seems the same, maybe excessive television or too much work or too much wasted time has prevented you from seeing the small pleasures around you.

Sample some of God's variety. If you're always up or to bed at the same time, maybe change things just a little to see a new angle. Get up ten or fifteen minutes earlier and walk outside, seeing the new morning light and savoring the quiet before the rush of the day begins. Or if your lunch routine is getting monotonous, bring a book or a short magazine article and really put yourself into it.

Third, think about your attitude toward everyday life. Is it one of appreciation for the gift of life, or is it one that says that nothing is ever right. On earth, nothing ever is perfect; that is reserved for Heaven, so if we are inclined to find fault, we can. Matters get even worse, when we complain. Have you ever noticed that complainers attract each other?

In our families, we need to strive to see the best in each situation, and help others see that as well. In doing so, we will be striving to see God. And seeing God in our present circumstance, even a little, is sure to make us happy.

The Family Vacation

Summer Vacation. Every school child yearns for this almost from the moment the Christmas lights get packed away. As February turns into March, the weeks until school's out are counted with care. Soon, the buds and flowers of Spring permit the counting to turn to days, rather than weeks, and before you know it, there are the kids at the door, with rumpled sheaves of paper and dog-eared books ready to embrace summer.

Those first few days go fairly well, until Johnny or Susan is unable to play or it gets so hot that no one wants to do "anything" any more. At this point, a certain irritability sets in, and Mom and Dad start counting the days until school starts again.

Some families conquer these doldrums with elaborately planned vacations to far-off places. While these can be good, they can also be expensive. What's more, sometimes an elaborate vacation takes so much time to plan, that it seems more like, well, work, than a vacation.

We also find in our family that if something is announced in advance or announced too early, it gets over-planned, or at least, over-debated. One child wants to stop somewhere along the way when another doesn't. Before you know it, a vacation that we planned for fun becomes a labor negotiation. The best rule of thumb for us is spontaneity or, at least, parental secrecy. Surprise the kids one morning with the prospect of getting in the car for a simple day trip.

As for destination, we select a comfortable place within a day's radius of home. Distances are kept reasonably short, so no one tires of the car. And the distance is made to seem shorter by having all of us sing or play any one of a number of "quiz show" type games. Cars can be confining, but they can also be uniting; at least, that is, if the radio isn't blasting and every passenger off in their own separate walkman-induced world.

We're not the camping type, so we usually end up at a reasonably priced motel. A swimming pool helps here a lot, but there is something about just being away from all the details of home that makes staying in a motel—even one that is far from luxurious—an adventure.

At our destination, we usually explore the local restaurants or interesting church or government structures. Many times, what must seem like an ordinary park to the local citizens becomes the "discovery" of our simple trip. Parks are good for stretching out under the summer sun to read a story aloud or taste some of the fruit purchased along the way from farm stands.

We seldom send any fancy postcards from the tiny hamlets we visit. We ask our relatives and friends not to be offended, since we're simply too busy creating an indelible family postcard or memory of a summer when God blessed us.

You can do the same with your family. You should.

And When Not on Vacation ... "Choredom" May Cure Summer Boredom

Near the end of every summer, a great many parents I know hope for its swift and certain end. Tired of hauling children from one play-camp to another or from one swimming party to another; tired of hearing children whine that there is nothing to do; tired of siblings provoking one another over who left the bathroom in a mess, with none of the siblings rushing over to clean it.

Now, not all children are like this, but many have their moments, especially in the dog days of August when school threatens on the horizon, but the brain is so accustomed to its low summer voltage that thoughts seldom enter or emerge successfully.

There is a solution to this: chores.

Yep, good ole-fashioned household chores: mowing the lawn, cooking dinner, washing dishes, clothes, windows, floors. You know, all that stuff that Dad, and especially Mom, is still expected to accomplish whether it's summer or not.

The best time for parents to have children start chores is when their young, under eight or so. If you've ever noticed, God has made these innocents willing to undertake almost anything. Huck Finn may have convinced his pals that painting a picket fence was fun, but with youngsters under eight, just about any task can be made appealing.

There is only one secret: parents must participate. In other words, for chores to be viewed as fun, it takes a parental partner. If toy manufacturers only knew how much children yearn to hammer a nail with Dad or stir the flour with Mom, they would waste little time trying to find new toys to market for Christmas.

Older children, jaded by television indoctrination and far-too-many peers with far-too-little to do in their own families, are admittedly a tougher sell. Some parents are tempted to use allowances or specific monetary incentives, but this should be avoided. In addition to teaching life-skills, the point of chores is to help children understand how responsibility to family, and often to the large community as well, is not just money or "what's in it for me."

Often the sharing of burden can be mitigated in a family way. Laundry, for example, can be done watching a special video or ballgame, when the television would otherwise be off. Alternatively, parents can allude to special outings or other activities that are possible but only after the work is done.

Home is not just a place for entertainment. Families work, as well as play, together. Families need to instill good working habits in their children. Chores is the way to do it. You might even say that a faithful commitment to "choredom," if you will, is the best antidote to end of the summer boredom.

And think how anxious it will make the youngsters for school.

When Strikes Came in Threes—Baseball and the Family

Among my fondest memories as a young boy growing up in Chicago were those spring and summer days when enough money had been saved up from yard work and paper delivery duty to board a city bus for Wrigley Field. It only cost 12 cents in those days for a kid to ride the bus with a pass, and a bleacher seat at Cubs' park went for a dollar. And lest you think I am some kind of dinosaur, this was the 1950s and '60s. I guess, to some of you, that does make me slightly pre-historic.

As we would head to the ballpark in the back (best bumpy ride) seat of the bus along the gray apartment house fronts on Addison Avenue, my brother and I and our friends would chatter on about whether Ernie Banks was the greatest shortstop (later, first baseman) of all time or whether Ron Santo was fast enough to get those squarely hit balls down the third-base line.

Funny thing about baseball talk, it is almost always uninformed. The facts seem to matter less than the personalities of the players.

Ernie Banks—or Mr. Cub as he was called—was perceived by us as a true gentleman. His smile and good humor were ever present in the face of adversity, which, given the Cubs' performance then and now, seems to begin most every afternoon around 1:30 P.M. Personality. Uprightness. Good Character. Clean Living. Loyalty. Kids like these things in ballplayers, almost as much as parents hope for them in their children. Maybe that's why, even with Frank Thomas swinging the bat as proficiently as he did in the summer of '94, the most respect of that summer from the kids I know went to Ryne Sandburg, who had the presence of mind to work hard at being good, and when that was seemingly no longer possible, to honestly bid the game goodbye.

The baseball strike didn't sit well with the kids. As scrupulously as kids followed Thomas' hitting or Bere's pitching, they didn't know or frankly care much about salary caps or revenue sharing among large- and small-market teams. Who could blame them? These issues are for the bean-counters. And lest the Cub's Mark Grace and his fellow unionists work themselves into a lather too quickly promising the owners yet another strike, they might try to understand how to the average kid, as well as the average Joe working the line at the factory, economic justice has very little to do with whether the salary minimum is in the low or high six figures.

No, the strike was just another manifestation of families being priced out of baseball. The kids on the Addison Street bus in the 1950s never had a hard time getting a ticket on game day. We never dreamed that ballplayers gave a hoot over who got the revenue from those wonderfully silly Hamms beer commercials on WGN featuring the hapless Hamms bear. Today, game-day tickets are near extinction, and their cost are beyond the reach of just about everybody, except the lawyers and account executives who seem to populate the stands with their clients and paramours most afternoons. And as for money, the players and the owners seem bent on pinching every last penny for themselves.

Well, good luck to them. The world didn't end with the baseball strike. Health care was no less expensive and its reform no more comprehensible. O. J. Simpson's endless trial more than filled in the empty television hours.

It's a shame we never learned whether Lofton would have hit .400 or Griffey broken Aaron's record or Belle exceeded 200 RBIs with or without his corked bat. But then, like the corked bat itself, the shame was all on them.

You know, the kids probably benefited if the strike caused us to remember what we did on those days when we didn't have the dollar and 24 cents for the all-day, round-trip Wrigley excursion. Some kids may have even stopped watching the play of highly paid actor-entertainers and started playing ball down at the park themselves.

My brother and I used to do that, when we weren't asking Dad to throw us a few sinker balls in the alley, and the only strike we cared about came in threes.

Affirmations of Love in Marriage

We hear so much about divorce and the decline of marriage, here are some practical things that can bring strength to a marriage:

First, husbands need to more frequently manifest love for their wives. We tend to think of showing affection only on holidays or birthdays. But Hallmark has no corner on the affection market. A little note of appreciation for being a good mother, a compliment on a dinner deliciously prepared, an offer of help with shopping or laundry can remind your wife how important and respected she is in the life of the family.

Wives too can repay the compliment, by taking their husbands seriously. Dad may come home with complaints about a problem at work or a concern over the cost of something, and it helps enormously to have a willing listener. Listening doesn't make prices any lower or problems disappear, but it makes them easier to face when you know you are not alone.

Problems or irritations are inevitable between spouses. Accept them as inevitable. When arguments arise, don't make them "federal cases," or generalize and lump them together with old, stale grievances. Problems will snowball if you let them, but it is better to handle these as they arise.

Children need time. Take a look at your day. Are your hours spent helping a child learn how to ride a bike or find the answer to a difficult math problem, or are they consumed by television or work or friends? Involve your child, even when work needs doing. If food shopping has to be done, take the children along, and give them part of the list of things to find on the shelves. Oh sure, going to the supermarket is not the same as going to Great America or Wrigley Field, but it is important time together.

Parents also need to spend some time with each other apart from the children. Parenting is tough work. Sometimes a break is needed. This may mean a night at the movies or a dinner out, but you know, some of the nicest evenings my wife and I have spent together have been on leisurely walks pouring out our hopes and fears to each other. A little conversation at day's end or before the ruckus of the day begins is well worth the time.

Finally, and most importantly, pray and pray regularly. In Deuteronomy, God tells us to love God with all our hearts and with our soul and with all our might. But more, He tells us that we must teach these things "diligently to our children, and shall talk of them when we sit in our house, when we walk by the way, when we lie down, and when we rise up."

A marriage built on regular affirmations of love between spouses, and between parents and children, and between family and God is sure to last a lifetime.

Maybe even forever.

Selected Bibliography

Adler, Mortimer J. *Six Great Ideas*. New York: Macmillan, 1981.

Ball, William Bentley. *Mere Creatures of the State?* Notre Dame, Ind.: Crisis Books, 1994.

Bennett, William J. *The Book of Virtues*. New York: Simon & Schuster, 1993.

Berger, Peter L. and Richard John Neuhaus. *To Empower People*. Washington, D.C.: AEI 1977.

Blankenhorn, David, Steven Bayme, Jean Bethke Elshtain, eds. *Rebuilding the Nest*. Milwaukee, Wis.: Family Service America, 1990.

Brownson, Orestes A. *The American Republic*. New Haven, Conn.: College & University Press, 1972.

Carr, David. *Educating the Virtues*. New York: Routledge, 1991.

Carlson, Alan C. *Family Questions*. New Brunswick, N.J.: Transaction Publishers, 1985.

Carter, Stephen L. *The Culture of Disbelief*. New York: Basic Books, 1993.

Catholic Parent Magazine, Our Sunday Visitor, Huntington, Ind.

Chapman, John W. and William A. Galston, eds. *Virtue* (Nomos xxxiv). New York: New York University Press, 1992.

Darling-Smith, Barbara. *Can Virtue be Taught?* Notre Dame, Ind.: University of Notre Dame Press, 1993.

Den uyl, Douglas J. *The Virtue of Prudence*. New York: Peter Lang, 1991.

Dobson, James C. *Focus on the Family Magazine*, Colorado Springs, Col.

Eberly, Don E. *Restoring the Good Society*. Grand Rapids, Mich.: Baker Books, 1994.

George, Robert P. *Making Men Moral*. New York: Oxford, 1993.

Glendon, Mary Ann, *The Transformation of Family Law*. Chicago: University of Chicago Press, 1989.

Guinness, Os. *The American Hour*. New York: Free Press, 1993.

Hunter, James Davison. *Culture Wars*. New York: Basic Books, 1991.

Hunter, James Davison. *Before the Shooting Begins*. New York: Free Press, 1994.

John Paul II. *The Splendor of Truth* (Veritatis Splendor). Boston: St. Paul Books & Media, 1993.

John Paul II. *The Apostolic Exhortation on the Family*, Familiaris Consortio. Boston: St. Paul Books & Media, 1981.

Klubertanz, George Peter, *Habits and Virtues*. New York: Appleton Century Crofts, 1965.

Kornhaber, Arthur, M.D., and Kenneth L. Woodward, *Grandparents/Granchildren— The Vital Connection*. New York: Anchor, 1981.

Murray, John Courtney, S.J. *We Hold These Truths*. Kansas City, Mo.: Sheed and Ward, 1960.

Neuhaus, Richard John. *The Naked Public Square*. Grand Rapids, Mich.: Wm B. Eerdmans, 1984.

Nisbet, Robert A. *The Quest for Community*. New York: Oxford, 1953.

Pennock, J. Roland and John W. Chapman, eds. *Voluntary Associations* (Nomos xi). New York: Atherton Press, 1969.

Rice, Charles E. *Fifty Questions on the Natural Law*. San Francisco: Ignatius, 1993.

Rockford Institute. *The Family in America*. (periodical)

Russell, William H. *Teaching the Christian Virtues*. Milwaukee, Wis.: Bruce, 1952.

Sears, William, M.D. *Christian Parenting and Child Care*. Nashville: Thomas Nelson, 1991.

Shaffer, Thomas L., *On Being a Christian and a Lawyer*. Provo, Ut.: Brigham Young University Press, 1981.

Sheedy, Charles E., C.S.C. *The Christian Virtues*. 2d. ed. Notre Dame, Ind.: University of Notre Dame Press, 1951.

Wilson, James Q. *The Moral Sense*. New York: Free Press, 1993.

About the Author

DOUGLAS W. KMIEC, is professor of law, University of Notre Dame and former Assistant Attorney General of the United States (legal counsel to President Reagan).

In addition to being a nationally known constitutional lawyer, Professor Kmiec is well identified with issues affecting the family. While in government, Professor Kmiec assisted the White House task force on the family and was instrumental in helping to write what is still regarded today as a "blueprint for family renewal."

Since leaving government in 1989, Professor Kmiec has addressed audiences from New York to California, as part of the distinguished Hesburgh lecture series, on the challenges and opportunities confronting the American family. His balanced, yet clear-eyed, instruction has also been very well received on a twice-weekly radio program—"The American Family Perspective." An energetic and effective speaker, Professor Kmiec has been honored as Notre Dame Law School's "Teacher of the Year."

Most importantly, however, as he demonstrates throughout this book, Professor Kmiec takes being the father of five children very seriously.